Foreign Affairs
Brexit and Beyond

Council on Foreign Relations

PRAISE FOR *BREXIT AND BEYOND*

"Yes, Brexit was a revolt against recent globalization and liberal cosmopolitanism. But it was also a product of the United Kingdom's long and ambivalent relationship to Europe. To understand why it happened, you have to read the *Foreign Affairs* collection *Brexit and Beyond*. It offers both first-rate, up-to-the-minute analysis by leading experts and a historical context and perspective that all the media frenzy on this summer's events can't provide."

—Mark Blyth, Eastman Professor of Political Economy, Brown University

"The essential guide to a transformative event."

—Anand Menon, Professor of European Politics and Foreign Affairs, King's College London

"An essential collection of articles on where Brexit came from, how it happened, and how it will change Europe forever."

—Henry Farrell, Associate Professor of International Affairs, George Washington University

TABLE OF CONTENTS

THE ROAD TO BREXIT

AFTER THE EARTHQUAKE

Introduction

Gideon Rose

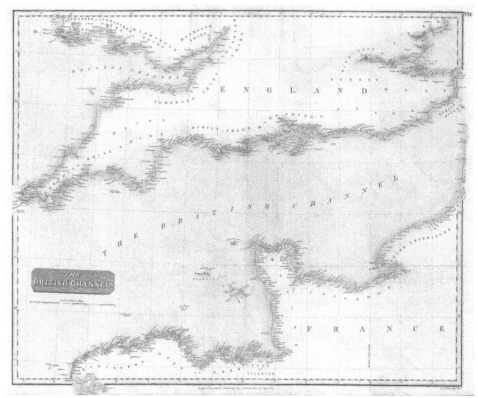

J. Thomson's 1814 map of the English Channel.

So close, and yet so far away. ...For thousands of years, the peculiarities of geography have shaped the relationship between the British Isles and continental Europe. The Channel and the North Sea have served as both barrier and bridge, creating a unique situation in which life on either side of the water has evolved neither entirely separately nor entirely in sync. After World War II, questions of political and economic integration displaced questions of military security, but how to share peace and prosperity has proved almost as difficult as how to avoid war.

Introduction

The shocking vote for "Brexit" on June 23 is thus only the latest twist in a long and complex story, and it raises far more questions than it answers. What does sovereignty mean in the twenty-first century? How much globalization is enough? And above all, is it possible for partners such as the United Kingdom and the European Community to remain loosely tied together in perpetuity, moving neither forward toward marriage nor backward toward divorce?

At Foreign Affairs, we've been following these debates closely for generations and are delighted to offer readers a guide to the subject that is as comprehensive as it is timely. It's all here: from the tussle over whether the United Kingdom should join the Common Market, to its unique role in the European Community, to the bold new era of the European Union, to the buildup of populist tensions in the wake of large-scale migration and the financial crisis, to the domestic political maneuvering behind the referendum, to the vote's stunning outcome and its turbulent aftermath.

We've gathered the highlights of our coverage from the 1960s to last week, all marked by the combination of authority and accessibility that is the hallmark of the Foreign Affairs brand. In June, Justice Secretary Michael Gove—one of the leaders of the "Leave" campaign—dismissed the overwhelming elite consensus opposing his position by saying, "I think people in this country have had enough of experts." If you agree with him, read no further. But if you want to understand the real issues at stake, how we got here, and what will happen next, this collection—supplemented by the ongoing coverage on ForeignAffairs.com—is for you.

GIDEON ROSE is Editor of Foreign Affairs.

© Foreign Affairs

Britain, the Six and the World Economy

William Diebold, Jr.

When France and Germany, with Italy and the three Benelux countries, made it clear that they were really going to form a customs union, they forced the British government to face a decision it had hoped to avoid. Now Britain's decision to join the Common Market, if reasonable terms can be agreed on, requires the United States to make some major decisions of its own. Our action-or the lack of it-will pose new choices for the rest of the world.

The British decision followed a long reexamination of the courses open to the United Kingdom once the Six had left little doubt-especially by their decision of May 1960 to accelerate tariff reduction-that they would succeed in creating a common market. Conversations in Europe, including those following the Adenauer-Macmillan talks of August 1960, presumably gave the British a reasonably good idea of the terms they would have to meet if they chose to go in. On the assumption that the Europeans would concede some essential points, the Prime Minister worked at building popular support at home and a majority in the House of Commons of a size appropriate to so fundamental a decision. The explicit opposition that remains-strongest at opposite ends of the Tory and Labor parties but scattered throughout the country-will undoubtedly gain recruits as a result of some of the compromises the government will have to make as a condition of entry. Concern for the Commonwealth will also influence votes. Still, the decision to seek entry could hardly have been made except in the belief that in the end the fundamental conviction would prevail that in the future Britain will be better off in the new Europe now taking shape than outside it.

Of course it takes two-or in this case seven-to make an agreement. Though the major champions of European integration have always said they looked forward to the time when Britain, and others, would join the Six, there has been opposition to British entry on the Continent as well as in Britain. Many confirmed "Europeans" were long opposed because they believed the British would undermine the European Economic Community, either in pursuit of a traditional balance-of-power policy or, less deliberately, because their Commonwealth preoccupations would inhibit full acceptance of European solidarity. No doubt this suspicion still lingers, but the British turnabout has been drastic enough and the progress of the Community substantial enough to silence most doubts, at least until it is seen where the negotiations lead.

A second main source of opposition to British entry lies in France. There the economic rationale for keeping the British out has largely faded, but France still aspires to be the main spokesman for Europe and does not welcome competitors. It is unlikely, though, that Frenchmen of these views- or Germans who have similar ideas, for that matter-would in the end stand out against a Community majority favoring British entry. Both sets of views- "European" and more traditionally nationalist-are likely to make themselves felt in a stiffening of the conditions that Britain will be asked to accept.

The three main sets of problems to be dealt with in the negotiations that have begun in Brussels concern Britain itself, its fellow members of the European Free Trade Association (EFTA), and, most important of all, the problems of the Commonwealth. How these problems are dealt with is crucial to the place of the enlarged European Community in the world economy.

II

During the years that Britain was in the wilderness so far as European integration was concerned, it was often advised that the way to set things right was to "accept the Treaty of Rome." That seemed an oversimplified view to those who were aware of the intricate set of compromises among national interests-and particularly between France and the others-with which the broad ideals of that document had been embroidered. Still, largely because Britain comes late and as a petitioner, it has virtually had to accept the existing rules so far as its own economy is concerned. "… We accept without qualification," Edward Heath, the Lord Privy Seal and chief British negotiator, told the Ministers of the Six, "the objectives laid down in Articles 2 and 3 of the Treaty of Rome, including the elimination of internal tariffs, a common customs tariff, a common commercial policy and a common agricultural policy." Gone is the argument for tariff autonomy and the established British tariff structure with its low duties on raw materials and foodstuffs that played so great a part in the British proposals of 1956 for a free-trade area. Heath made it clear that the British would not question most of the rates already agreed on for the common external tariff but asked that duties be eliminated on aluminum, woodpulp, newsprint, lead and zinc, which the United Kingdom now imports free, largely from the Commonwealth. (Benelux and Germany already have the right to import substantial quantities of some of these materials duty-free in spite of the common tariff.) On such matters as social security laws, regulation of business practices, taxes, and rules covering the establishment of foreign business, the British have asked only for time to adjust their arrangements to those called for by the Treaty. They know that as members they will have a voice in determining how the broad principles of the Treaty are to be applied in these matters.

Agriculture once seemed a great hurdle. Although Mr. Heath spoke about it at length in presenting Britain's case, he was mostly asking for time to make adjustments. The British seem to have decided some time ago that they could afford to switch from their system of relatively low prices and subsidies for farmers to the continental one of price supports. Consumers will pay more; the treasury will pay less and gain some customs revenue; overseas sellers may get higher prices. Though the present disposition in Britain is to minimize the cost of the change, there is room for some concern about the effect of higher living costs on wages. What this part of Britain's entry price comes to will depend to an important degree, in the short run, on the arrangements made for the importation of Commonwealth foodstuffs and, in the long run, on the influence Britain will have on the common agricultural policy of the Community.

EFTA, conceived to a considerable extent as a collective bargaining device, has become something of a problem for Britain in its new posture. Denmark and Norway will probably follow Britain into the Common Market. Portugal's rather limited trade problems are not expected to be troublesome. The difficulty centers on Austria, Sweden and Switzerland which send a high proportion of their exports to the Common Market but are not prepared to join it because so many of its leaders stress its long-range political purposes. The Austrians say the Russians would forbid their joining. The Swiss say their neutrality would be compromised. The Swedes say much the same and put themselves forward as a necessary bridge to Finland; but there is a significant minority in Sweden that favors entry. What the three "neutrals" would like is a form of association that would give their exports easier access to the Common Market without involving them in commitments on other matters. They are meeting resistance from some of the leaders of European integration who see this as a dilution of the Community at a moment when British accession makes it particularly important to stress solidarity and the obligations of membership. The British are involved in the problem because they have virtually committed themselves-by an agreement that will sooner or later invite charges of bad faith-to delay joining the Common Market until the interests of the other EFTA members are satisfied.

The problems of Britain's relations with the rest of the Commonwealth are even harder and more numerous. In the first instance they concern trade-a large volume of trade. Most of Britain's imported food comes from the Commonwealth. The economies of Canada, Australia and New Zealand have been shaped to a significant degree by the importance to them of the United Kingdom's market for grain, meat, dairy products and fruit. If Britain were simply to step behind the common tariff of the European Community, long-established trade patterns would be disrupted. Dominion products that had previously entered the United Kingdom freely would encounter tariffs. The tariff preferences that now favor the Commonwealth would be replaced by others favoring European products. When the Community's common agricultural policy became fully operative (if it followed the lines now contemplated), Commonwealth foodstuffs, like those of the rest of the world, would be subjected to variable levies intended to limit imports to the amounts the Community could not produce for itself with an expanded agriculture.

Tropical Commonwealth producers have different problems. With the major exception of sugar, their competition is usually not in Europe, so the common agricultural policy is of little importance to them. Some of their products face no tariff barriers; taxes on coffee, tea and cocoa that hold down sales of these commodities to the Continent will not be affected by British accession. But some Common Market tariffs exist for the purpose of giving preferential treatment to the products of the African countries associated with the Community by virtue of their former colonial affiliations. If Britain entered with no special arrangements, it would levy a tariff on cocoa from Ghana but not the Ivory Coast, and on peanut oil from Nigeria but not Senegal.

The advanced countries of the Commonwealth, and especially Canada, sell relatively small but growing quantities of manufactured goods to Britain. Tariff preferences, which are generally supposed to be particularly important for this trade, would be lost if Britain joined the Common Market, and replaced by a preferred position in the U.K. market for manufactured goods from the Six. Some underdeveloped Commonwealth countries send cheap manufactured goods to Britain, where they are treated far more liberally than in the continental countries (or the United States). There has been remarkably little public worry about what British entry into the Common Market might do to one of the most sensitive parts of this trade-the export of cotton textiles from India, Pakistan and Hong Kong. Perhaps there would be no great change since present tariff rates are less important to this trade than import quotas on the Continent and export restrictions which the Commonwealth countries apply on shipments to the United Kingdom. Also, negotiations are under way for a multilateral agreement on cotton textiles that might widen continental markets for Commonwealth producers. This is, however, only the first installment of what promises to be a major trading problem of the future as developing countries increase their exports of cheap manufactured goods.

There is little doubt that the Six will agree to arrangements which will protect some parts of the Commonwealth's trade structure. But other segments will inevitably be subjected to new barriers and some degree of discrimination as Britain eliminates tariffs on imports from the Continent and adopts the common external tariff. British participation in the Community's common agricultural policy is bound to affect Commonwealth trade, but how much depends on whether the prices set for Community producers lead them to expand output enough to displace Britain's imports from the Commonwealth and whether the preferences of British consumers will be strong enough to persuade them to keep buying such things as Canadian hard wheat at higher prices than they have been used to.

All these changes will be introduced in stages, over a period of years. If the British economy should respond to the stimulus of the Common Market by growing more rapidly than it has in recent years, imports of Commonwealth products might expand in spite of the new pattern of trade barriers. Moreover, the Community's external tariff is going to be subject to international negotiation during the years ahead. Commonwealth countries will have the same chance as the United States to bargain it down. The addition of Britain is likely to strengthen the low-tariff forces in the Community. Of course, trade is not the Commonwealth's only concern. An expanding British economy might be better able to provide capital for development. A paper prepared for the Third Afro-Asian Economic Conference in New Delhi suggested another point when asked, "Is not the stability of sterling a better cement than the maintenance of 'preferences'?"

Even if British entry into the Community brings substantial economic benefits to the Commonwealth in the long run, will it also strengthen the Commonwealth as a political system? Considering the imponderables by which the Commonwealth lives, and the ability it has shown in one decade to accept conditions that seemed impossible in another, one would be foolhardy to give a flat answer. Perhaps the course of the negotiations will give us an idea of what calculation Whitehall has made about the long-run future of the changing Commonwealth and Britain's chances of continuing to lead it while also joining Europe-a feat once held to be impossible. Clearly, one of the main tasks of British diplomacy must be to hold on to as much influence in the Commonwealth as it can. It would surely defeat that purpose for Britain to enter the European Community with no concessions for Commonwealth trade. But it is unlikely the Six will refuse some special measures, at a minimum to ease the transition but perhaps also with a view to establishing new trade relations between the Commonwealth and Europe.

III

There are a number of different ways in which the problems posed by Britain's entry into the Community might be handled. While it seems improbable that Canada, Australia or New Zealand will apply for membership, one or another of them might seek some form of association with the Community to improve its access to the European market, as the EFTA neutrals are doing. Britain has already agreed to let the Dominions negotiate away its preferential position in their markets and some have thought the thing to do was to extend these privileges to the Six in return for enlarged European purchases of foodstuffs. Tariff-free quotas or minimum-purchase guarantees of some sort are likely to be used as transitional devices and may also be proposed as lasting arrangements, not only for food but for some Commonwealth raw materials as well, if the Community rejects the British proposal to reduce these tariffs to zero.

One way of dealing with the problems of Africa would be to give the British dependencies and former British territories the same privileges as the former French, Belgian and Italian countries have in relation to the Community. An alternative would be to put all the underdeveloped countries of Africa, Asia and Latin America on an equal basis, providing their major exports with equal access to the markets of all the industrialized countries of the free world, as Alfred C. Neal proposed in Foreign Affairs in January 1961. In relation to the EFTA countries the question is whether to apply the same simple choice-in or out-that has been applied to Britain or to accept the view that a different political situation justifies a more limited kind of special agreement tailored to meet the problems of the European neutrals.

These "solutions" differ greatly in their economic and political implications. The concessions they would require by one side or the other vary widely. Quite a few of them are not compatible with GATT-the General Agreement on Tariffs and Trade. Some of them clearly enlarge the area of free or liberal trade while others mostly give one nation a preferred position at the expense of another.

This spill-over of European economic integration creates great problems for outside countries and may do much to shape the whole free-world trading system. The pressures to get agreement without disturbing existing trade patterns too much are bound to encourage special deals and other arrangements that in substance if not in form give certain countries preferred positions in the European market. If the arrangements are only temporary, no one need worry too much, so long as he is sure they will in fact be terminated soon. Otherwise, integration in Europe may lead to fragmentation in the economy of the rest of the free world.

It is a little hard to believe that the long-run interests of the free world are advanced if Australian meat can be sold to Britain and the Continent on more favorable terms than meat from Argentina or if coffee growers in the Ivory Coast are given privileges denied to those in Uganda, while Brazilians and Colombians have to cope with entirely different marketing problems. The rule of equal trade treatment embodied in GATT is not just a relic of the nineteenth century or an idealistic premise nurtured in back rooms in Washington by postwar planners. The departures from it that could be sanctioned in good conscience in the postwar period have been justified, as in the case of European integration, by three criteria: the dollar shortage, the achievement of long-run political benefits or the ability of a few nations to go substantially further in breaking down barriers to trade among themselves than would have been possible for a larger group. The dollar shortage is over, so far as Europe is concerned, but the others remain rather good tests, whether the question is one of granting Austria special status, assuring a market for Canadian wheat, or either adding Ghana to the Common Market's associated states or subtracting Dahomey from them. It makes quite a lot of difference, too, whether the special problem is met by measures that discriminate between one country and another or by concessions directed toward the special needs of one but extended equally to others. To a considerable extent the application of GATT rules will meet these standards and GATT provides the best place for discussing hard cases and departures from the rules. But it will be largely up to the "outside" countries and particularly the United States to insist on this.

IV

The new critical phase in Europe is one to which American policy has contributed. We have encouraged European integration, tried to strengthen the Community, and hoped it would expand, at least to include Britain. To reverse that policy now would be nonsense inviting chaos. If the British decide to throw in their lot with the Community, we should welcome the result for what it will do for the political strength, balance and orientation of Europe. To cope with the resulting problems we have only a limited choice of policies.

Quiescence has not much to recommend it. If the United States were to stand by, waiting, the Six, Britain, the Commonwealth and the remaining countries of EFTA would probably work things out. The price in terms of American economic interests might be high and we would probably have missed the chance to use the period of flux in Europe to move decisively toward a better ordering of the free world.

An active policy does not mean a once-for-all action. If the United States sets out to play a major part in shaping the changes that have been set in motion, we shall have to be prepared for a long process of dealing with a large number of more or less discrete problems in as coherent and consistent a fashion as we can manage. Our power abroad will be limited; to use it we will often have to overcome domestic inhibitions of the sort that arise when pursuit of the general interest damages particular interests. This means we will be involved in struggle and compromise and will have to accept inadequate and unsatisfactory measures a good part of the time. This is nothing new, but it will make trouble if we do not have a clear idea of our direction and aims.

American policy should have three purposes: to encourage the success of the negotiations between Britain and the Six; to minimize the short-run economic costs to the United States of British entry into the Common Market while opening as many chances as possible of economic gain for ourselves over the long run; to take advantage of the processes of change being set in motion by Europe to improve the organization of the free-world economy. The last two purposes may sometimes conflict with the first since we shall be asked to put up with arrangements we dislike or disapprove of on the grounds that they are necessary to get an agreement in Europe. There is no general solution to that dilemma but it is worth remembering that fuzzy, temporizing arrangements sometimes offer the best chances of change later on.

The pursuit of the second and third aims will often ran along a single course. It has been obvious for a long time that it is important to the United States to have the Community's tariff on our exports as low as possible; with Britain added, this will be all the more true. Regardless of one's views on the particular points of President Kennedy's trade-policy proposals, there can hardly be any serious doubt that only by a major step of this sort can the United States hope to be effective in furthering its export interests and preventing the negotiations for British entry into the Common Market from spawning a series of special arrangements that might do much to disintegrate the free-world economy.

We should have allies in this course. Japan, Latin America, the unaffiliated countries of Asia and Africa, European outsiders, and, on many occasions, the members of the Commonwealth have interests similar to our own. Canada, with its striking postwar record of pursuit of a multilateral trading system, has been tempted by the view that "lying low right now is our best tactic," as The Financial Post of Toronto put it. Fortunately, the mood seems to be changing as it becomes clear that Canada is unlikely to get very much of a free ride as a result of American and British bargaining with Europe, and that meanwhile things will be decided in which Canada will want to have a strong voice. It is important that the outsiders see their common interests, for if each country felt forced to come to whatever terms it could with the new Europe, each would be likely to seek arrangements partly at the expense of the remaining outsiders, and real disintegration would set in.

Some people have supposed that the best way out of a difficult position would be for the United States to "join the Common Market." This is hardly a meaningful statement. Addition of the United States would so transform the Common Market-in size, scope and character-as to make it something else. Hence the talk of an Atlantic free-trade area. There is a strong case for the view that free trade between Western Europe and North America would, after a period of adjustment, strengthen the whole area and make these countries better able to meet their triple need of providing for defense, satisfying the wants of their people and contributing to the economic development of the underdeveloped countries. But the United States is plainly not nearly ready for so drastic a step, and the Europeans are probably not ready for it either. Some would fear a check in the progress toward Western European integration. And if we were all ready, it would be most unwise to create an Atlantic free-trade area before Europe and the United States were substantially agreed on measures that would help the other countries outside the Soviet bloc meet their trade needs.

One of the great advantages of the Kennedy Administration's trade program is that it provides means of dealing with immediate problems without foreclosing the possibility of an eventual free-trade area between the United States and Europe. By concentrating on tariff bargains between the United States and the Community, the program would reduce the significance of our being outside the Common Market. By stressing adherence to most- favored-nation tariff treatment, by both the United States and Europe, the proposals make it possible to spread these benefits to other countries and, more importantly, maintain the essential principle that what is to be built is a trading system of benefit to the whole free world and not just to a rich white man's club.

This argument does not reject the idea of an "Atlantic Community." NATO, the Marshall Plan and the O.E.C.D. all show that the affinities and common interests of the countries around the North Atlantic provide a basis for fundamental cooperation on a large scale. That these countries need to find still more effective ways of concerting their policies seems obvious. For some purposes "Atlantic" is plainly a misnomer. Measures already taken to coordinate foreign aid include Japan; that country as well as Australia, New Zealand and others undoubtedly should have a place in other "Atlantic" activities as well. It is particularly important that they should not be excluded from trade cooperation since they have a major stake in the markets of Europe and North America.

If the time comes when Europe and North America are ready to create a real free-trade area, they should seek the broadest possible membership, tested by willingness to participate, not location around the shores of the Atlantic. Before then the industrialized countries can take steps to improve the trading position of the underdeveloped countries. One measure already under discussion would remove import barriers on a number of tropical products. Measures might follow to replace the preferences some African countries have in Europe with equal treatment for these and other countries in the markets of the industrialized countries. Measures to help offset the fluctuations in income of raw-material exporting countries would also be more effective if Europe, North America and Japan worked together with all the producing areas. A special effort will be needed to work out effective and acceptable arrangements to provide markets in the advanced countries for cheap manufactured goods from low-wage areas.

Combined with tariff concessions on a most-favored-nation basis and a strengthening of GATT-instead of the erosion that will come in the absence of a deliberate policy to support that body-steps of this sort will make it possible to move toward freer trading relations inside the "Atlantic Community" while at the same time improving the trading position of the rest of the world. This may also provide ways of meeting the problems of European countries that remain outside the Common Market. One thing it will do little to solve is the agricultural problem.

The agreement among the Six on the principles of a common agricultural policy was a major step in extending the scope of the Community. What its economic effect will be is not entirely clear and depends to a considerable extent on the support prices that are established and the way they are financed. The new policy will probably promote a greater degree of self- sufficiency in a number of farm products. It will certainly add to the difficulties of overseas countries that export food to Europe. Normal import liberalization, already very limited in agriculture, is made virtually impossible by the new policy. For some time to come the United States, the Commonwealth countries and others will probably be able to make specific arrangements for the sale of their products, but it is hard to see how they can have much assurance about the long-run future under the new system. The management of domestic agricultural economies in which almost all countries now engage is forcing increased management of international trade in farm products. But how this is to be done, and what the economics of it will be, remain obscure. The question is one more major addition to the agenda of international economic cooperation.

Quite apart from the agricultural problem, the United States will not find it easy to pursue the course called for by our new situation. We are unaccustomed to the requirements of a vigorous trade policy entailing adjustments at home. But if there is one lesson to be learned from Europe's recent experience it is that advanced economies can function remarkably well without their traditional tariff protection. The position of the United States is not the same as that of the European countries. Sluggishness in the economy, our newfound balance-of-payments difficulties, and the need to maintain an exceptionally large export surplus to meet overseas commitments all hamper us. A vigorous trade policy cannot stand by itself, but a reduction of import barriers should contribute something to the solution of all these problems, not least by its effect on costs of production.

If the United States takes this course we are not likely to pursue it simply and constantly, with no setbacks. If we do not move in that direction we are likely, in a very real sense, to be left behind. Europe's trade dynamism is coupled with economic strength. If the United States is inactive, Europe's needs, desires, preoccupations and compromises will do more to shape the free-world's trading system than will our own. Europe's decisions that created this situation were in an important degree made possible by the policies the United States followed after the war. Now they pose new policy choices for the United States.

© Foreign Affairs

After Brussels

ANDREW SHONFIELD

Participants hold a British Union flag and an EU flag during a pro-EU referendum event at Parliament Square in London, Britain June 19, 2016.

In 1962 the European enthusiasts in Brussels were explaining regretfully that although British membership would slow down the process of European integration-perhaps severely impede the whole movement toward a United States of Europe-it was a price that had to be paid for widening the geographical spread of the Community. No doubt these people, while regretting the manner of General de Gaulle's rupture of negotiations with Britain, are now privately relieved that the price will not have to be paid. Their view is that Britain's inherent weakness is such that she will be compelled sooner or later to come back and knock on the door again and plead for entry into the European Economic Community (E.E.C.). On the whole, better later than sooner. The European Community will by then have consolidated itself; it will be able to impose its terms with less difficulty and, in fairness it should be added, will be less niggling about making small concessions which may contravene the letter, though not the spirit, of the Treaty of Rome.

All told, then, in the view of this school the British negotiation was premature. It was forced on the Community by British diplomatic pressure and carried forward almost within sight of a successful conclusion as a result of British diplomatic skill. Only a major coup in the contemporary rough diplomatic style of the French could have stopped it. That it was the French has some incidental advantages. Having been so rough with their own partners and caused them much loss of face, the next moves from France, it is argued, must surely be placatory. And one sure-fire way in which de Gaulle could placate the offended Europeans would be to offer to speed up the process of European integration. The end product in that case could therefore be an offer of more supranational powers to the European Commission in Brussels. Thus, in spite of Voltaire and the recurrent and variegated manifestations of the astringent French spirit, all may still be for the best in the best of all possible worlds.

The argument rests on two major assumptions: first, continuing British weakness and sense of isolation; second, steadily growing cohesion and strength in the European Economic Community. As to the first, it is quite true that the ground swell in favor of joining the Common Market, which affected a wide segment of British public opinion, was partly prompted by the sense of national disillusion. There was the discovery that the special relationship with the United States was not after all very special; that the position of leadership in the new Commonwealth was more a matter of ritual than of substance; and, above all, that the traditional methods of managing British economic affairs seemed to be grossly and irretrievably inefficient by comparison with the group of West European nations which habitually set themselves ambitious economic tasks and then fulfilled them. However, it would be wrong to suppose that Britain was simply waiting for membership in the E.E.C. to tackle the various problems that had contributed to this sense of failure. On the contrary, since 1961 there have been a number of important initiatives in different fields of British domestic policy designed to prepare the ground for a series of fresh starts. Outstanding among these are the creation of the new economic planning organization, the National Economic Development Council, which has now produced an elaborate five-year program of accelerated growth; a drastic scheme for the reorganization of rail transport on a nation-wide basis; and moves toward an overhaul of the whole system of agricultural support.

The truth is that joining E.E.C. would have provided the occasion for putting over these and other radical changes of policy, with the help of an appropriate supporting political fanfare. But the act of joining would itself have solved nothing. At best it would have served to make the compulsion to act quickly exceedingly obvious. The failure to get into Europe could now, if skillfully exploited, be used to make it only a little less obvious. The significant point which may be overlooked is that British policy has evolved in the course of the 15 months of negotiation in Brussels-and earlier in the course of reaching the decision to negotiate-to the point where the country and the Government are ready to accept decisions which would have been barely conceivable not so long ago. Just take one example: having contemplated the complete elimination of tariff protection for a number of extremely tender British industries, other measures which involve awkward competitive pressures no longer terrify. One immediate practical consequence is that the tariff reductions on goods coming from EFTA countries[i] are to be speeded up, and probably eliminated altogether by 1966. Having traversed a lot of fresh and interesting ground in the approach to the E.E.C., the Government plainly has no intention of going backward.

Perhaps the most striking thing in London immediately after the breakdown in Brussels in February was the absence of any sensation of rebound. The Government gave no encouragement whatsoever to the people who were calling for a sharp turn toward the Commonwealth; nor did it countenance any recriminations with the Common Market. One or two small gestures of displeasure toward France were all that the Government permitted itself- little enough in view of the fact that the major plank of its present policies and future election program had suddenly and brusquely been knocked away by the French President. It is known that the British Cabinet did briefly consider the possibility of démarches and ritual fuss on a large scale, and the idea of bringing in the United States to put pressure on the European Community. Certainly the United States was willing to help. But the view which finally prevailed in London was that nothing should be done which might prompt the Six to draw demonstratively together against anything that looked like an Anglo-American initiative. Throughout, British policy has remained ostentatiously European, not only in direction but also in method.

Looking ahead, the series of British economic measures which started last autumn and reached their climax in the budget tax reliefs in April suggest that the Government is set on a policy of economic expansion. Assuming that the Government means what it says when it promises not to be panicked this time into acts of restriction by a sudden balance-of-payments crisis, it is by no means clear that, say, by the end of 1964, the British economy will look either unprosperous or feeble. There is no mystery about the causes of the economic stagnation and high unemployment of last winter. They were the result of deliberate policies-perhaps a better description would be self- inflicted wounds-chosen in 1961-62. These policies have now been sharply reversed.

Britain will of course suffer certain economic disadvantages through exclusion from the Common Market. But there are offsetting gains which are not inconsiderable. British exporters are in an exceptionally favored position in two groups of markets, EFTA and the Commonwealth, which together take more than twice the amount of the British trade that goes to the European Common Market. Moreover, in these sheltered markets (responsible for nearly 45 percent of her export earnings) Britain has no serious industrial competitor such as there would have been inside E.E.C. Admittedly neither of these trading blocs is as dynamic as the European Community, but it is worth noting that at least in one of them, EFTA, Britain will benefit in the period ahead from the increasing discrimination against the goods of competitors like the Germans. That should allow Britain to capture an increasing proportion of the business done in EFTA markets and offset the prospective loss of business in E.E.C.

II

The future of British policy toward Europe will of course be influenced largely by what happens inside the European Community itself. The evidence so far, on the basis of the short period since the breakdown of negotiations in Brussels, suggests two things. First, the Six are not going to remain stubbornly split; there is enough consensus to allow decisions to be carried out in a number of fields of economic and social policy. But secondly, there is no sign that France is prepared, as the European optimists hoped, to pay some sort of penalty for its intransigence toward Britain by making special concessions to the European Community. Nor is there evidence so far of any abatement of General de Gaulle's hostility toward the aggrandizement of the European Commission, which is the heart and the essence of the E.E.C. He has previously dealt summarily with the supranational pretensions of one Frenchman in Brussels, Etienne Hirsch, by having him dismissed from his post as President of EURATOM. Another, Robert Marjolin, who is a vice president of the European Commission, is an open opponent of the Gaullist régime. It should always be remembered that the top officials of the Community are appointed for a four-year term only, that their jobs are in the gift of national governments, and that they will in the end be no more European and supranational in spirit than each of their governments encourages them to be.

All this is relevant to the prospect of achieving more cohesion among the Six during the period ahead. The Six are now facing a series of difficult decisions on major issues which will be solved only if governments are prepared to take risks involving their political future at home. It is unlikely that they will do this unless they are given a clear guarantee of reciprocity which they can show to their own electorates. The most obvious example at the moment is the set of decisions which have to be reached on the E.E.C.'s common agricultural policies. For the first time in the Community's history, governments-notably the German Government-are asked to accept the prospect of a serious sacrifice of electoral advantage; that would surely be the consequence if several million peasant voters were told that they must henceforth expect a large reduction in the guaranteed prices for their produce. This is a different kind of test from anything to which ruling parties have been subjected in the past. The mood of the participants, and above all the presence or absence of the mutual trust which comes as a result of the assurance of reciprocity, is in such circumstances all-important.

Dr. Gerhard Schroder, the German Foreign Minister, has in effect demanded that France demonstrate its good intentions. At the beginning of April he told the Council of Ministers that in Germany's view the Community's effort had been excessively concentrated on agricultural policy, which France regards as the sine qua non of further progress by the Community, and that there must now be mutual concessions in other equally important spheres of policy. It is possible that France will eventually give the sign that is asked of her. But there are other issues waiting to be tackled outside the field of agriculture, where agreement will be just as hard to come by. For instance, the complicated and ambitious proposals for oil and coal-where the interests of the Six are widely divergent-await action. More profound is the issue of economic planning for the Community as a whole; the German opposition to any such exercise, whether on a national or a European basis, has been raised in a sharp form by the European Commission's Program of Action for the Second Stage.

Indeed it can be argued that the impression of increasing cohesion which the Community has given in the recent past owes a great deal to Britain. There is no doubt that the British negotiation with E.E.C. was a potent instrument for compelling agreement among the Six on difficult issues like agriculture. Some of the concessions to French views made by France's partners were certainly intended by them as a contribution toward the concurrent bargaining with Britain. At that stage the negotiation with Edward Heath supplied a kind of linchpin for the Six. The British negotiators had a more difficult time in consequence, for once the Six had agreed among themselves they became extremely rigid. It is, however, questionable whether the Six will be able to build much, in the immediate future, upon the agreements provisionally reached among themselves in the course of the negotiations with Britain. In this respect Britain almost certainly got the better of the bargain: the negotiations pushed Britain into making a number of decisions on policies which are unlikely to be reversed, whereas no comparable residue has been left behind for the Six.

There is of course the possibility that some fresh external pressure will fulfill the same function for the Common Market that Britain performed in 1961-62. At one stage it was thought that the Kennedy Round under the Trade Expansion Act might indeed fulfill a dual purpose: on the one hand, force a coherent external policy on the European Community; on the other, help Britain, by bringing European tariffs down, to repair some of the damage caused by her exclusion from the Common Market. But subsequent feelings both in London and in Brussels are that the Trade Expansion Act will probably prove to be a far less powerful instrument for international negotiation than the Americans originally thought. In spite of the eagerness of Walter Hallstein and the European Commission to take advantage of the opportunity now offered, the E.E.C. countries led by France are likely to demand from the United States firm commitments which the Administration will find it hard to give.

It is a mistake to imagine that the demands which are likely to be made on the American negotiators in the Kennedy Round are exclusively a French design to make life more difficult for another branch of the Anglo-American family. France is to a large extent acting as the spokesman for doubts which are widespread in the Common Market. The essential point which the whole incident underlines is that it has by now become exceedingly difficult to treat tariff negotiations as a thing on their own-in the traditional style-without bringing all sorts of other matters, often of a domestic character, into the argument. At the very least that is likely to impose a limit on the mutual concessions that will be made in the Kennedy Round. If, however, the French decide to press their point to extremes in order to keep the common external tariff of the E.E.C. inviolate, it might be more serious than that. This has led to suggestions in Brussels that an effort should be made to strike a bargain between the French and the other members of the Community, tying an agreement on the E.E.C.'s agricultural policy to the tariff negotiations with the Americans. In its simplest and most optimistic form, the idea is that the French should be offered an attractive deal on agriculture on condition that they agree to bring forward the date of the Third Stage of the Common Market, which is not due for another two and a half years. The significance of the Third Stage is that decisions on tariff changes will then be made by the Council of Ministers on the basis of a qualified majority (instead of unanimously as now), which means that France could no longer impose a veto on a big bargain in the Kennedy Round.

Once again, the characteristic feature of this scheme is the hope that France can be brought to accept a deal with a European price tag attached to it. Needless to say, this type of proposal is regarded with no enthusiasm in London. Indeed, the British fear has been that the United States Government might become so obsessed with the desire to make a splash with the Kennedy Round that it might induce the friendly E.E.C. countries to make unfortunate concessions on vital issues to the French point of view. The alternative, as it is seen from London, is for the E.E.C. members to stand pat until the Third Stage of the Rome Treaty, and if necessary delay any serious tariff negotiations with the United States until the Community can make its decisions by qualified majority voting. That will happen at the end of 1965, and no action by France can now stop it. It would be foolish to bargain away anything of importance in order to gain a short extra period of lower tariffs.

The standpat argument can of course be applied more broadly, taking into account the various other fields of European policy in which the unanimity rule will give way to qualified majority voting in the not very distant future. Indeed, tactically it has certain attractions for the extreme European integrationists, as well as for the British. It could be used as a means of bringing home to the French that there are a number of acts of further integration in Europe which will take place anyhow. France can no longer impose a veto on the progressive limitation of national sovereignty in these particular fields; the right to do so was surrendered when the Six passed from the First to the Second Stage of the Rome Treaty in January 1962. This fact, if firmly pressed home with a policy of no-blackmail-by- France, might then persuade the French Government that its wisest course, after all, would be to accelerate the process of integration and thus recapture the good will of its partners in the E.E.C.

But if the tactical pressure failed to produce the desired result, would the European leaders in Brussels be prepared to face a period during the next two and a half years in which the momentum of integration in all major spheres, other than tariff reductions, was drastically slowed down? That seems most improbable. After all, the central doctrine of the Treaty of Rome is that tariffs cannot be isolated as a separate compartment of national policy; making a customs union in modern conditions necessarily involves a wide range of other decisions taken in common. But an even more potent consideration would be the psychological effect on European business of a period during which the machinery of integration was retarded. It is a familiar point that the success of the European Community to date owes a great deal to the fact that businessmen have anticipated the realities of the Common Market in their own business decisions. They powerfully assisted European integration, because they were convinced that integration would occur. And they were convinced in large part by the practical evidence of the "Community spirit" among the governments which consented to the stream of decisions emerging from Brussels. Now, it is not being suggested that they would promptly reverse their positions if the stream were turned into a thin trickle. But they would surely be inclined, over a period, to hedge their bets more and more on European integration; and one simple way of hedging is to delay.

III

All this is another way of saying that integration is a highly cumulative business. The maintenance of visible tempo is the first essential. It follows that for all the initial tough talk of some of the Brussels leaders, like Dr. Sicco Mansholt, a vice president of the European Commission, they are likely in the end to be ready to make very extensive concessions to the French viewpoint in order to maintain the appearance of momentum. However, the more important question-since integration is only given shape in Brussels, but has to be willed elsewhere-is whether the national governments will be prepared to follow suit. I have already mentioned reasons for doubting whether they will. One of the key issues in this connection is the treatment that will be accorded to the permanent British delegation at Brussels; and this brings the argument back again to the future of British policy. It now looks as if the British Government, having considered and rejected a variety of possible devices to fill the post-Brussels gap, has plumped for a reinforced diplomatic mission to the Six which by its presence will constantly assert Britain's special relationship with the Community. While this may seem a flat and disappointing conclusion to the whole affair, the arrangement could have more important consequences than appear at first sight.

The Six have, after all, stated it to be their policy to ensure that the E.E.C. and Britain shall consult closely on matters which might impede any future attempt to negotiate British entry into the Community. Secondly, it has been suggested that Britain herself should try to ensure, so far as possible, that EFTA and E.E.C. move in step with one another on major decisions of policy. Plainly, Britain and the Scandinavian countries at least are going to try to use EFTA as a means of providing some compensating trade advantages for the increased discrimination that will be exercised against them by the E.E.C. With the further EFTA tariff cut scheduled for July 1963, the total reduction will amount to 60 percent, which is large enough to make German exporters to Scandinavia feel the draft. There are, therefore, good commercial reasons, quite apart from political considerations, why the German Government should be anxious to establish a formal arrangement which will keep EFTA and E.E.C. in regular and intimate contact.

It is not clear at this stage how far Britain is planning to go in reinforcing EFTA and using it as an instrument of international trade policy. There has been talk about a possible attempt to "harmonize" the external tariffs of the EFTA countries, at present widely different from one another; such a move would clearly help the group to operate from a position of much greater strength in any world-wide tariff negotiation. But any serious attempt to convert EFTA into a more closely integrated group, with common institutions analogous to those of E.E.C., comes up against the objection in London that the interests of the members are, in fact, too disparate to fit easily into a single harmonious system. No doubt something more will now be made of EFTA than its British founders, at any rate, originally intended. But it is unlikely to set itself up as a rival community to E.E.C.

Potentially, the most important consequence of keeping a powerful British mission in Brussels is that it could provide the means of consolidating the relationship established between Britain and five members of the Six during 15 months of negotiation. Whether it will in fact produce this result depends partly on how seriously Britain takes the whole enterprise and partly on the energy which the Community countries are prepared to apply to the business of consultation. There is no doubt that the Benelux representatives and the Germans are in earnest about it at this stage. If the British coöperate by producing a mission of the right type, the practice of close consultation on the details of E.E.C. policies as they develop could quickly become rooted. For practical purposes it would be a continuation in another form of the dialogue which developed between the British delegation and the E.E.C. representatives during the later stages of the negotiations in 1962. Moreover, it would be more difficult for France to sabotage the process of consultation than an actual negotiation, and there would be no question of a veto.

It is possible to conceive of day-to-day consultation of this type becoming so intimate and close as to be barely distinguishable from the making of joint decisions. A formal hearing in the meetings of the Council of Ministers would be unnecessary-just as the United States Ambassador, in the heyday of the Anglo-American special relationship, required no access to British Cabinet meetings in order to ensure that the American Government's needs and wishes were a potent factor in shaping relevant decisions. However, the content of the relationship envisaged with E.E.C. will be very different from the Anglo-American one, since it will specifically involve the domestic policies of both sides-something which the British and the Americans have always been at such pains to avoid. If, for example, the E.E.C. wants to go ahead with a common energy policy, the relevant questions on which agreement will need to be reached will include the size of the British subsidy, if any, to be paid to unproductive coal mines; the home price of coal charged by the National Coal Board; the amount of the excise duty levied on oil; the countries from which oil is to be imported and perhaps the quantity of stocks to be kept in storage. Just as the whole Common Market technique has involved systematic mutual interference in the domestic affairs of member countries, a successful attempt to keep a non- member marching in step with the Community must involve the same kind of interference-from both sides. One consequence of this form of consultation would be to complicate and delay still further the already difficult process of reaching agreement on major policy decisions in E.E.C.-a tendency which the European Commission, guardian of the tempo of the Common Market, can be expected to oppose. Quite reasonably, the Commission would point out that the E.E.C. was having the worst of all worlds-by allowing an outsider an influential voice in decisions for which he bears no ultimate responsibility. If the system is to work, the central idea of the E.E.C., which is the unremitting search for a fresh consensus in a constantly wider range of policies, must willynilly include the outsider. The real problem is that almost any decision which welds the existing members closer together, e.g. over agriculture, is likely to carry E.E.C. and EFTA further apart. To keep the two blocs moving in parallel with one another, as they have done so far in their timetables of tariff reductions, will not prevent them from excluding each other's trade. The temptation therefore will be to delay such decisions.

All this assumes firstly that powerful consultative machinery between Britain and E.E.C. is established, and secondly that the Six are unable to agree among themselves on an ambitious new program of accelerated European integration. If they were, in fact, able to agree-more specifically, if France were willing to accept a major sacrifice of national sovereignty-the group would almost certainly refuse to allow the imperatives of European union to be trammelled by any commitment to an outsider like Britain. Consultation would have to wait. If France turns out not to be ready to pay the price, then the prospect is that in, say, two years from now Britain will not be faced with a tight and ever more coherent Community, but with an entity which is still fundamentally as loosely knit as the E.E.C. is today-and whose looseness is much more apparent. The process of formal integration, which puts a compulsion on national governments to subordinate their own decisions on important matters to a collective will, is much less advanced than is often imagined. Britain's adhesion to the E.E.C. in 1963, with the obvious sacrifices of national and Commonwealth interests which this would have entailed, would have powerfully reinforced the mood making for more rapid European integration. There is no comparable compelling force now in sight. A loose Europe would of course be a club which Britain would find it easier to join-though from the point of view of a British European it would be far less worth joining.

[i] The countries of the European Free Trade Area are Austria, Denmark, Norway, Portugal, Sweden, Switzerland and the United Kingdom.

The European Community and 1992

STANLEY HOFFMANN

Taking a glass of champagne after signing the Draft Treaty on European Union, Cavaco Silva, President of European Parlament, Dutch Ruud Lubbers, German Hans-Dietrich Genscher and French Jaques Dalors in Maastricht, Netherlands on February 7, 1992.

Not much attention was paid in March 1985, when the European Council, whose members include the chiefs of state and government of the 12 member states, decided that it should constitute a single market by 1992. After all, the European Community had been established in 1957 with the goal of a common market, and many people believed that the goal had been reached; tariffs within the Community had been abolished, a common external tariff put in place and a controversial common agricultural policy instituted.

Those who knew better realized that Europe remained a maze of border controls, government subsidies to national industries, closed national systems of procurement in military and other key public sectors, and national regulation of industrial standards, copyrights, transportation, banking, insurance and health requirements for the entry of goods. Thus, many were discouraged; after all, the goal of a full economic union had been proclaimed in the early 1970s but never met.

Americans in particular had been enthusiastic about European unity in the 1950s and 1960s-often more so than many Europeans-because they had a vision of a United States of Western Europe, symbolized by the name of Jean Monnet. They grew disheartened when Charles de Gaulle, in the 1960s, was able to destroy that dream and force his partners, in the so-called Luxembourg compromise of 1966, to stick in effect to the rule of unanimity. The Community settled down into one more international organization in which diplomats and bureaucrats haggled over technicalities. American curiosity moved to other parts of the world.

By 1988 it had become evident that this time, something new had indeed happened in Western Europe. Three months after the council's 1985 decision, the European Commission, which is the executive branch of the Community and consists of 17 officials selected by the national governments but independent of them, published a White Paper that listed no less than 300 areas for action, with deadlines for proposals by the commission to deal with them. Ever since, the commission has been turning out directives, and the Council of Ministers, which takes most of the final decisions, has examined and usually adopted them. It was the White Paper that set the deadline of 1992 for the achievement of a truly common market. By the middle of 1989 about half of the obstacles had been removed-or at least ordered to be removed.

The task undertaken by the Commission of the European Community (EC) is both gigantic and intensely technical. Progress so far has consisted of such measures as the replacement of the hundred-odd forms required of the members' citizens at European borders by a single administrative document; the directive of June 1983 that provides for the mutual recognition of professional qualifications-a measure that should allow engineers and doctors (although not lawyers, who will need to take an exam in the country into which they move) to settle anywhere in the Community; another decision to eliminate the remaining controls on capital movements; a directive that allows a bank, licensed in its home country, to operate throughout the Community; a decision to remove restrictions on road transportation; various moves aimed at the deregulation of European civil aviation (whose fares are much higher than U.S. fares); a 60-page directive on the regulation of engineering machinery, and another one that liberalizes the terminal equipment market-a sector each country had heavily protected. Funds that support the poorer countries of the Community have been doubled, and represent the equivalent of the Marshall Plan. The commission is also playing a very active role in antitrust cases, a role which entails opposing mergers that have anti-competition purposes or ordering governments to stop subsidizing firms illegally.

The ultimate beneficiaries of all these measures are likely to be both the producers and the consumers. Border controls alone cost between three and four percent of total trade in 1983. A truck that could travel 750 miles in Britain in 36 hours needed 58 hours to cover the same distance from the Channel to Milan. Changing money into local currencies would cost a traveler going to ten of the 12 member countries 47 percent of his money. The closed character of public procurement is another important cause of high prices, especially in computers and telecommunications. If the council and the commission continue their efforts, European industrialists will achieve economies of scale that will allow them to operate more efficiently than if they were confined to their domestic markets, and the consumers will gain from the commission's competition policy, which is strongly supported by the jurisprudence of the European Court of Justice.

II

What explains this sudden burst of activity? A few years ago, it was fashionable to lament about "Europessimism." Suddenly "1992" has become the symbol of a European renaissance. It can best be explained as the conjunction of a common experience and of key personalities.

The experience was that of the Community's dark age-roughly from 1973 to 1984. In 1972, three years after the resignation of General de Gaulle, who had opposed Britain's entry into the Community, Britain became a member. Many people had expected its very capable officials, many of whom were fervent "Europeans," to take the lead and inject new vigor into the Community. Instead, there followed more than ten years of quarreling about the amount of money Britain had to contribute to the EC's budget-Britain in essence asking for a renegotiation of the terms on which it had been allowed in.

Moreover, when the oil crisis of 1973 hit, the Community was incapable of agreeing on a common policy; most of its members followed America's leadership, with France dissenting. It suddenly appeared that many of the economic problems that plagued Western Europe could only be solved on a global level, and that the Community's regional framework was irrelevant. Finally, the economic slowdown of the 1970s, with the rise of massive unemployment, led the governments to ignore the Community and give priority to strictly national, and often divergent, attempts at coping with the crisis-through alternations of expansive and restrictive fiscal policies, and such measures as what the French called "the social treatment of unemployment": retraining, subsidies to firms willing to hire new workers, unemployment compensation and so forth.

The result was a sense of failure. The national policies had only limited success; there was little growth, excessive inflation and persistent unemployment. During these years Japan became a major economic actor, and the new industrial countries of Asia followed Japan. Europe witnessed the decline of many of its traditional industries, such as steel and shipbuilding, and discovered that in many areas of high technology it was being outpaced by Japan as well as by the United States. Attempts by governments (especially that of France) to promote mergers of firms so as to create "national champions" in such areas as telematics did not succeed in reversing the trend. Governments, after years of trying to improve their national economies through such attempts and through deals with unions and business organizations, became aware of the rigidities of the labor market as well as of the many other obstacles to industrial efficiency and technological progress. If national solutions did not work, there remained one way out: what the French often call a fuite en avant, an escape by a forward leap-into Europe. Competitiveness on the global market remained the main issue, but now it appeared that regional integration was, after all, the prerequisite.

Nonetheless, Europe would not now appear so promising if, during the "dark years," steps had not been taken to preserve the Community from decay and to strengthen it in some important areas. The most significant and successful effort was the establishment-after several false starts-of the European Monetary System (EMS) in 1978. It was the brainchild of West German Chancellor Helmut Schmidt and French President Valéry Giscard d'Estaing.

The abrupt American decision to scuttle the postwar system of fixed exchange rates and to replace it with floating rates had worried the Europeans, who were afraid of the effects of monetary instability on their trade and balance of payments. The EMS provided for a tighter system than the global one; fluctuations of exchange rates were to be contained within a narrow band (known as the "snake"). Even though Britain did not join, it cooperated with the EMS, which has tended to be a Deutschmark zone. The main merits of the EMS have been its contribution to the reduction of inflation and the pressure it puts on the governments, if not to coordinate their fiscal and economic policies, at least to follow similar ones, under the surveillance exerted by various Community committees. Bonn's policy of monetary stability has become the continental norm. When the Socialist government of France in 1981-83 tried to pursue a Keynesian policy of public spending to counter the recession, French balance-of-payments difficulties and the run on the franc quickly forced it to choose between quitting the EMS and reversing its policies- and it did the latter.

Another measure of progress during those years was the Esprit program, a scheme of industrial cooperation in information technology promoted by the very able Belgian Commissioner Etienne Davignon with the collaboration of the 12 major electronic companies of the Community, and with Community subsidies. Still another prerequisite for the future leap was the settlement of time-consuming disputes over British money, over the budget, and over the Common Agricultural Policy, the reform of which was finally undertaken in 1984 to make it less expensive (it absorbs 70 percent of the Community's budget) and less wasteful (the reduction of butter stocks and of the production of wine being the priorities).

Thus, by 1984, the members had overcome many obstacles. Moreover, disenchantment with Keynesian policies, the wave of economic liberalism spreading from Reagan's America (particularly the appeal of deregulation), the recognition by French and Spanish Socialists of the superiority of the market over a command economy, of the futility of nationalizations and of the virtues of competition-all this created the right climate for the European revival. Just as in the 1950s when the Christian Democrats of France, Italy and West Germany turned to "Europe" partly as an escape from the limits or frustrations of their domestic policies, the Socialists of France, Italy and Spain-followed in 1989 by Britain's-found in "Europe" a substitute for their traditional public policies at home.

However, general conditions only lead to the right results if the right people are in the right place at the right moment. This is what happened in 1984-85.

After the fiasco of his first economic and social policy, French President François Mitterrand, an old "European," was determined to use the six months of his presidency of the European Council in 1984 to make spectacular progress. The new German chancellor, Helmut Kohl, could only view with favor a plan that would, on the whole, benefit West Germany's strong industry. Prime Minister Margaret Thatcher, as an apostle of deregulation, had no reason to resist, and was also eager to prove that Britain was not the saboteur of the Community it had often seemed to be. The Single European Act-whose long-term effects, as the ratification debates showed, were probably underestimated by all the governments-was presented to the British Parliament as a treaty that would make it possible (by majority votes) to bring to Western Europe all the benefits of deregulation, while preserving (through the requirement of unanimity) national sovereignty in areas essential to Britain, such as taxation, the free circulation of individuals and the rights of workers.

Above all, the new president of the EC Commission-the person whose impetus can be decisive-was Mitterrand's former Minister of Finance Jacques Delors, who had been a key adviser to the reformist Gaullist Prime Minister Chaban-Delmas in 1969-72 and later became a moderate Socialist. He had been very influential in turning around the economic policies of Mitterrand's government in 1983. A former official of the French labor union inspired by progressive Catholic thought, he exemplifies the synthesis of Christian democracy and socialism on which the Community was built. His commitment to a United Europe is as strong as his obstinacy and energy. Delors, who was reappointed for a second four-year term last year, is as important to the enterprise today as Jean Monnet was in the 1950s.

III

This new enterprise builds on the institutions and achievements of the earlier one, but it is not a mere continuation. A comparison of the two efforts is instructive.

The Common Market of 1957 was limited to six neighbors: France, West Germany, Italy, Holland, Belgium and Luxembourg. The first European experiment was a reaction to what academics sometimes call "high politics"-considerations of national security and power. The Coal and Steel Community of 1951 was launched as a way of promoting the reconciliation of France and Germany and of anchoring the one-year-old Federal Republic in the Western alliance. The European Economic Community was established by the 1957 Treaty of Rome after the fiasco of the European Defense Community, which was scuttled by the French National Assembly in 1954, and after the humiliation of the British and French during the Suez crisis of 1956. In both instances, the six members chose economic means to reach political objectives-the ability to speak with one voice in world affairs-because these means prompted less internal resistance and because the whole realm of defense was dominated by the United States. Indeed, the main underlying issue-the one that de Gaulle, between 1958 and 1969, made brutally explicit-was the ability of the Six to stand up to, distinguish themselves from, and cooperate as an equal with the United States.

Throughout the 1950s and 1960s this issue became entangled with a quasi-theological debate about the Community's institutions. Jean Monnet, the "inspirer" (de Gaulle's rather hostile term) of the 1950 and 1957 enterprises, supported a sort of federal setup-limited to the economic sectors covered by the 1957 Treaty of Rome-with the independent EC Commission as its chief body. The Common Market of 1957 diluted Monnet's dream by making the council of state representatives the real decision-maker and by creating a parliament that was not elected by universal suffrage nor provided with any real powers (the switch to universal suffrage a few years later did little to enhance its authority). De Gaulle excommunicated federalism (called "supranationality" in Monnet's euphemistic jargon) by insisting on the primacy of the council and on the principle of unanimity for decisions. He saw in Monnet's design a danger that French sovereignty would be destroyed by irresponsible "European" bureaucrats, whom the United States could manipulate by exploiting the clashes of national interests among the six countries.

De Gaulle preferred a "Europe of states": a concert of governments that would build "Europe"-first in the West, ultimately in the East as well-on the basis of well-balanced bargains in areas of common or mutual interests. So did Britain, but de Gaulle kept it out of the Community on high politics grounds: Britain's closeness to Washington. Finally, the first European enterprise remained limited in scope (as well as geographically); agriculture and the removal of tariffs and quotas on trade were the only links forged among the Six.

The post-1984 undertaking is very different. Today the Community has 12 members and is far more heterogeneous. With Portugal, Greece, Spain and Ireland in the Community, 20 percent of the member countries have a per capita income inferior to 60 percent of the average; in other words, it has a "North" and a "South" of its own. The EC Commission-de Gaulle's target after 1958-has been a major actor, as has been the new European business elite fostered by the Common Market's removal of some barriers. In the 1950s many businessmen, especially in France, were very hostile and fearful of the project. The main goal now is not "high politics" but the competitiveness of Europe in a world in which the number of industrial and commercial players has multiplied; the stake is what Helmut Schmidt once called the struggle for the world product, rather than for traditional power (although wealth and power have become ever more closely tied together).

While the United States remains a major trading partner of the Community, the new effort is aimed much less at establishing a "partner" of equal weight to cooperate with, and to resist domination by, the United States than at resisting the challenge from Japan, whose aggressive external economic expansion and fierce protection of its own market the Europeans resent. This shift in emphasis reflects the relative decline of American power.

The theological battle about the Community's institutions is not dead-Jacques Delors is the new Monnet and Margaret Thatcher the new de Gaulle in this connection-but it has been suspended and replaced by a remarkable pragmatism. In 1985 Europe's statesmen did not follow the federal path favored by Alfiero Spinelli's draft treaty of European Union, which the European Parliament had endorsed in 1984. They preferred the goal of a single market to the straight path of political integration. To be sure, the Single European Act signed in 1986, which amends the Treaty of Rome and endorses the commitment to a unified market, allows for decisions in most areas to be taken by a qualified majority instead of unanimously, but the European Council remains the top decision-making body.

The earlier supranationalists often saw the states as the enemy; today's activists see them as indispensable partners, whose sovereignty is to be pooled rather than removed, and to whom enforcement of Community decisions is entrusted. There is also, now, an impressive network of national and transnational lobbies in Brussels and Strasbourg (where the European Parliament meets), of experts' and bureaucrats' committees advising the commission and the council, and of ties among cities, regions and enterprises. The scope of the Community is larger, thanks to the EMS and to the mass of joint ventures, cross-border mergers and direct investment abroad that now tie the members together.

Some things, however, have not changed. The political motor of the Community remains the Franco-German entente; when it sputters, progress stops; when it functions, advances are made (because Britain wants to avoid being isolated). As in the first effort, the members find it easier to agree on removing obstacles than on formulating common policies (which would require greater powers for the federal bodies-the commission and the parliament). The best example of this is the set of principles adopted for the unification of the market. One principle-stated by the Court of Justice in a 1978 case that pitted the French liqueur cassis de Dijon against West Germany-is that the members would grant each other "mutual recognition" of their regulations and standards, i.e., the conditions set in one country have to be accepted by the others. The other principle is home-country control: the right of a firm to operate throughout the Community if it is licensed in one of the member countries. These principles make it unnecessary for the commission and the council to spend too much energy on "harmonization"-the adoption of a single European set of standards-or on promoting "European" companies. There will be instead a kind of free market of competing national standards.

Another similarity between the earlier effort and the current one concerns the dynamics of unification. Neither effort has been accompanied by a popular, mass movement. In the first enterprise, there was often considerable domestic opposition (witness the fate of France's own brainchild, the European Defense Community, in France); the moves toward integration were the product of a small layer of key politicians and civil servants. Today, these actors and the business elite are driving the effort, and, as shown by the high rate of voter abstention (about 41 percent) in the June 1989 elections for the European Parliament, the general public is not very involved. This lack of interest may be because the European bureaucrats have been clever enough to bury the controversial issues under a mountain of 300 technical directives and because the parliament, despite its new powers (granted by the Single Act) of amending council decisions and approving agreements of association between the Community and other states, continues to appear remote and bogged down in technicalities. The election campaigns were much more about domestic politics than about Europe.

Furthermore, in neither effort has the nation-state necessarily "lost" whatever power was "gained" by Europe. The main winner has not been a supergovernment of Europe; the national governments and bureaucracies remain the chief players, for instance setting up and revising the Common Agricultural Policy and very actively taking part in the mergers and collaborative schemes devised (or merely executed) by firms.

A final similarity is that the European enterprise remains primarily economic. Efforts at coordinating foreign and defense policies-the former under the auspices of the European Council, the latter mainly through the West European Union, a sleepy organization set up in 1955 as a substitute for the Defense Community-have remained fitful and limited.

IV

To these limits must be added the other difficulties the new undertaking faces-difficulties which guarantee that the year 1992 will not see the full realization of a unified market. What has begun is a process that will go on for many years, and which is galvanized by but cannot be bound to the artificial deadline of 1992.

The method pursued in Brussels has the advantage of appealing to the desire of all groups for expanded production and trade at lower prices, and of leaving to the future the determination of the losers. Enormous interests are at stake, for this massive attempt at deregulation will provoke shifts in wealth and therefore power among nations, regions, classes and sectors that nobody can yet fully forecast, but that create anxieties and resistances galore. There is the fear that the results will amount to the victory of the richer countries over the poorer ones (hence the fierceness of the battles over the size and distribution of the funds granted to the poorer nations, such as Greece) and of the richer sectors over the poorer ones (hence the disgruntlement of farmers, whose income is falling despite the costly agricultural policy). There is also the fear that the new Europe will represent the triumph of the most efficient and powerful economies over the others.

The story of the EMS is one of West German preponderance; Bonn has preserved its trade surplus with its neighbors despite the upward movement of the Deutschmark because their currencies have moved up along with it. France and other members of the EMS often fear that having lost mastery over their monetary and foreign economic policy, they will have to take measures curtailing their economic growth (hence increasing unemployment) in order to remain within the EMS and preserve the equilibrium of their commercial balance. French industry, which has, on the whole, smaller firms and less available capital than West German industry, and which has begun playing the game of internationalizing itself rather late, worries that the removal of all barriers within Europe will flood the French market with foreign imports. On the other hand, the heavily protected and not very efficient West German transport and telecommunications industries may be the losers in the unified market. And Italy fears that Italian capital, when controls are lifted, will move to countries that provide higher returns on savings, and thus stop financing Italy's public debt.

Labor is afraid that the removal of barriers and increasing competition will lead to a large number of business failures and layoffs, and to businesses moving to countries with lower wages and social benefits such as Spain. The labor markets of Western Europe are far less integrated than the capital markets, and further integration would require a common social policy and collective bargaining on a Community-wide scale. But there is little governmental enthusiasm for such moves, which would disrupt delicate domestic balances and affect national competitiveness; policies for coping with this "social dimension" of Europe remain nebulous.

The attempt by the EC Commission to draft a statute for European companies has been plagued by disagreement over provisions for worker participation-West Germany objecting to anything less than the co-determination granted by its own law, and Prime Minister Thatcher rejecting any scheme that would boost the power of unions, which she fought so vigorously in Britain. Labor's sullenness contrasts with the frenzied activity of businessmen, who are engaged in formidable contests in the form of mergers, joint ventures, buyouts and takeover bids aimed at obtaining either the best position through transnational alliances in Europe or the best position in their country against the expected onslaught of competition from abroad.

These multiple fears and oppositions explain some of the setbacks and delays encountered by the pioneers of "1992." Attempts by the commission, prodded by Delors, to define a common social policy have not gone much beyond generalities and the recognition of diverse national practices, falling well short of the guaranteed minimum income that some labor organizations have called for. Plans for a Community-wide television broadcasting network have been stymied. Little progress has been made in matters of copyright and patents. Opening up procurement in the four traditionally protected "national" areas (energy, telecommunications, transportation and water supply) is only beginning.

The two most troublesome sectors among those covered by the White Paper have turned out to be border controls and indirect taxation (no attempt is being directed at unifying direct taxes).

The abolition of all border controls is fiercely resisted not only by customs employees but also by Prime Minister Thatcher, who believes these controls are indispensable in the fight against drugs and terrorism. Moreover, each country remains free to impose its own conditions on the admission of refugees and immigration-a very hot political issue, as the rise of Jean-Marie Le Pen in France has shown; the abolition of border controls would make the enforcement of such national policies far more difficult.

The unification of indirect taxes has hit a number of snags. One concerns the value-added tax; countries with low rates or very limited coverage for the tax (such as England) fear that raising the rate and increasing the coverage would be inflationary. On the other hand, France, which gets 40 percent of its public revenue from taxes on consumption, resists the loss of government income a lowering of its rates would entail. A compromise is now being negotiated; it would set only a common minimum rate, and Britain could retain its exemption of "social items" from the tax. Some members also oppose a reduction in the rates of "sin taxes" (on alcohol or tobacco). At the meeting of the European Council in December 1988 Mitterrand threatened to delay the lifting of controls on capital movements until a common scheme of taxation on interest and dividend payments was devised, so that French investors will not be tempted to send their money to countries where such taxes are low or applied only to residents. But after the Bonn government decided to scrap its domestically unpopular withholding tax on interest, the EC Commission's attempt to devise a common withholding tax collapsed.

In two important areas not covered by the White Paper, divisions persist, hindering progress. Many officials believe that the unified market will require a centralized monetary system, with a single currency (the European Currency Unit or ECU, which exists already but plays only a minor role in transactions) or at least fixed exchange rates between the national currencies, and a central bank. Otherwise, once capital movements are free, currency volatility might increase and put unbearable strains on the present European Monetary System. This drive is resisted both by Britain, eager to preserve some autonomy for the pound, and by the Bundesbank, which plays in fact the role of a central bank for the EMS and is, as a national bank, freer in its decisions than if it were transformed into the equivalent of the Federal Reserve for 12 countries. Moreover, the West Germans insist that any central bank would have to be independent of political authority-whereas the Bank of France is an instrument of government policy.

In April 1989 a committee headed by Delors proposed a three-stage plan toward full monetary union, but the European Council, meeting in Madrid in June, avoided a showdown with Prime Minister Thatcher by agreeing only to proceed with the first stage-reinforced cooperation in economic and monetary policy. It agreed to plan an intergovernmental conference to prepare the later stages (and to revise the Treaty of Rome to allow for the transfers of state power that monetary union would require). Such a conference would require unanimity to succeed. Ultimately, unless Britain's position changes, its partners will have to choose between a highly diluted version of the Delors plan and a union without Britain.

The other area in which sharp disagreements persist is "political cooperation," the code name for diplomatic coordination. At the council meeting in Rhodes in 1988 the 12 leaders were not able to agree on a common response to the new position of the PLO, even though, in the late 1970s, some progress had been made in establishing a common West European stand on the Arab-Israeli conflict. Nor has there been a unified response to Soviet leader Mikhail Gorbachev's initiatives and calls for a "common European house": French distrust, British caution and the West German wish for a new and generalized détente do not blend. Indeed, the desire of all three countries for some diplomatic autonomy will continue to set limits to diplomatic harmonization, and keep this area from being as successful as the path to the single market. But the increasing importance of economic issues in world affairs is likely to reduce the difference between the Community's well-established foreign economic policy and its shakier political coordination, as in the case of its relations with Eastern Europe.

V

These hesitations and divisions show not only that "1992" is going to be a long and difficult process, but also that the shape of the future European entity remains uncertain, dependent on the personalities of the main statesmen, on the economic situation of Europe and on the international political climate. The enterprise can proceed as long as there is, if not a common purpose, at least sufficient ambiguity to accommodate a variety of national purposes: Bonn's desire to find in the Community both a field of economic power and a legitimation of its links with the German Democratic Republic and of its Ostpolitik, France's intention of tying the Federal Republic solidly to Western Europe (in exchange for the reduction of French economic and monetary autonomy), Spain's will to become a major player in European affairs and to pressure its economy into efficient modernization, and Britain's enthusiasm for deregulation. But sooner or later these ambiguities will have to be clarified. At present there are two sets of uncertainties: internal and external.

The first internal one is the main object of debate between Thatcher and Delors. The British Conservative leader sees the new enterprise in the perspective of economic liberalism, as an exercise in removing obstacles to the free movement of people, goods, capital and services. Her Europe is a true common market, with as little governmental intervention as possible. In this respect, she is the heir of British policy in the 1950s, which aimed at the creation of a vast free trade area in Europe and established the European Free Trade Association (EFTA) with those continental West European states that had not joined the Six, precisely because the latter wanted to build a common entity.

Delors acknowledges that economic integration must precede social harmonization and that deregulation must come first. However, the French Socialist leader, who has devoted most of his public life to issues of social policy, emphasizes the need for joint actions, for a framework of European rules and institutions to guide and discipline the market and to prevent the social and regional injustices that unfettered competition-especially among gigantic firms and conglomerates-could produce. As he has often put it, "savage capitalism" is not his ideal; cooperation must temper competition and harmonization must complement the destruction of barriers. What is at stake is the extent to which the new Europe will be the preserve of businessmen and of the market-oriented conservatives, rather than a more social-democratic Europe in which public power will have a major role and workers will feel protected.

The second, and connected, internal issue concerns the institutions of the new entity. The deregulated market dear to Thatcher needs no other institutions than the present ones, and, indeed, requires that the central bureaucracy in Brussels remain weak. The trouble is that the main actors in this market, the business elites, may end up being accountable to no one, and in a position to manipulate both the national and the central bureaucracies that try, often competitively, to control them. Delors' vision is far more institutional; he wants if not greater powers for the European Parliament at least a more energetic supervision of Community decisions by the national parliaments, and above all more powers of enforcement for the EC Commission, so that its directives will not be disregarded by states with very strong bureaucracies (France) or states with very messy ones (Italy). He also wants increased independence for members of the commission; when a government doesn't like the activities of the commissioner it has designated, it can simply refuse to reappoint him, as Thatcher did in the case of Lord Cockfield, the author of the White Paper.

Against such a conception, Prime Minister Thatcher invokes the defense of British sovereignty, just as de Gaulle insisted on French sovereignty. (But he was more consistent: he believed in a highly interventionist state, whereas she believes both in the British state and in an open, unfettered market.)

What is at stake is the future of the nation-state in Western Europe. Delors' logic is ultimately that of the construction of a federal state, albeit one that would deal only with issues that the member states cannot resolve by themselves (this is the "principle of subsidiarity"). The transnational market would be accountable to the federal government. Member states would have extensive residual powers in areas such as education or justice, but the central institutions would regulate and supervise the common economy and ultimately the common defense and diplomacy. Legitimacy would be provided by universal suffrage, expressed in the election of the European Parliament.

Other "Europeans" who reject Thatcher's stand nevertheless hesitate to follow Delors. In truth, most governments find it easier to cede powers to the market than to a central government above them. If they prevail, the new entity will be a very original experiment indeed, a construction in which there will be extensive common functions, but functions carried out through bargains negotiated among and enforced by the member states, and where loyalty will remain centered in the nation, as it is today. (Open any European newspaper: national issues, and particularly the distinctive features of national politics, dominate the daily news.) At best loyalty will be split, unevenly, between the nation and a Europe with rather weak central institutions.

Whether such a confederal model could last is a fascinating question. Both the United States and the Swiss Confederation have moved from such a condition to a more federal, which means more centralized, state. But the differences among the 12 members go much deeper than those among the Swiss cantons and the states of the United States of America.

Some believe that the more the members are willing to pool and to share their theoretical sovereignty, the stronger will be the need to build up the central institutions, especially after Prime Minister Thatcher is gone. In this view, she represents, like de Gaulle, a transition between the imperial past and the European future, during which nationalism-combined with a pragmatic albeit distrustful view of European cooperation-serves to restore national self-esteem, a necessary prelude to any abandonment of sovereignty.

But others argue that the more the states' effective sovereignty shrinks, the stronger will be their determination to protect what is left of it, and to find ways of controlling the growth and direction of the institutions in Brussels. Some believe that the demands of the disadvantaged or victims of economic integration will lead to action at the Community level, others fear a strong national backlash-especially if redistributive efforts at the Community level are limited both by the size of its budget and by the constraints of the EMS.

The differences among the members will be even greater if the Community expands further and admits Turkey, the most recent candidate, and such possible new applicants as Norway and Austria. This raises the questions concerning the Community's relation to the outside world, the second set of uncertainties. Already, the Community has a wide and complex network of agreements with external associates in Europe, the Middle East, North Africa and a large number of former colonies in Africa, the Pacific and the Caribbean. The move toward a single market has placed on the agenda the problem of the Community's relations with the EFTA countries, with which it would like to make new arrangements collectively rather than having to deal with the separate demands (or applications) of the six members. The Community's members are reluctant to admit Austria because Austria's neutrality is seen as a handicap for the common diplomatic and defense policy of the future. Also, the European Parliament is on record against the admission of Turkey, whose demographic growth is deemed unmanageable in a Europe whose people could circulate freely.

The issues that excite Americans most are those of the external economic orientation of the enterprise. Will it be "Fortress Europe," a protected market, or will it be an open Europe? Clearly, the purpose of the whole effort is not merely to increase wealth by removing obstacles to production and technological progress, but also to increase Europe's power in a world in which economic and financial clout is as important as military might. The current transformation is aimed at making the penetration of external markets, through trade and investment, easier for European countries, many of which depend on exports for their growth and have capital available for placement abroad. It is also aimed at minimizing the penetration of the Community by forces deemed unfriendly. American entrepreneurs or officials are not the main targets (although France wants to curb U.S. programs on European television), but it is difficult to devise external barriers against Japan or South Korea that do not affect U.S. investors and companies as well.

The main bones of contention (in addition to such hardy perennials as the Common Agricultural Policy, which favors European farmers at the expense of American farm exports) are found in two sectors-neither of which is covered by the rules of the General Agreement on Tariffs and Trade, that somewhat graying Bible of free commerce (from which recent U.S. trade legislation departs considerably).

One is the domain of financial services. Foreign banks and insurance companies will be allowed to set up branches in the EC if reciprocity is granted by their country to European banks and companies. Americans are not justified in believing that this means the exclusion of American establishments because the legislation of certain states of the United States is restrictive. The Community has moved toward a very lax definition of post-1992 reciprocity; banks and insurance companies already operating in EC countries before 1992 will be treated as European.

Access of foreign companies to key sectors of public procurement is likely to remain restricted, however, even though American companies established in Europe qualify as European companies.

A third area of possible contention is the automobile industry. The Europeans want to keep Japanese car imports down as long as the Japanese market is closed to their cars, and they might impose a quota on cars produced in the United States with predominantly Japanese capital or a high content of Japanese parts.

A protectionist Europe remains unlikely, however, not only because of international legal obligations, but above all because of West Germany's and Britain's opposition, the many alliances between EC and non-EC (American, Swiss and Swedish) enterprises and the high level of European investments abroad. (In 1987, European companies invested $37 billion in the United States, but American ones invested less than $2.5 billion in Europe.) However, much will ultimately depend on the state of the world economy and on the behavior of the United States and Japan. All one can see at present is a tendency both in the United States and in Europe to give a more restrictive interpretation to the notion of reciprocity-one that looks at outcomes in specific sectors rather than at the fairness of procedures and at overall bargains. Also likely is the continuation, in Japan, of a strategy aimed at maximizing the global power of the industries in which it has the lead. A world economic recession could not only turn the world economy into a contest of protected regional blocs, but could also slow down the dismantling of barriers and definition of joint policies within the Community.

VI

The external economic orientation of Europe will also depend on the international political context. Until now, the cold war and the importance of the Atlantic alliance to the United States and its European allies have had a dampening effect on trade quarrels. The United States has tolerated what it sees as European protectionist measures because the prosperity of Western Europe was an overriding American goal, and the need to preserve the American military protection of Europe has often caused the Europeans to react with moderation to American economic demands or restrictions.

If the Soviet-American contest should cease being the most important issue in world affairs, conflicts of economic interest among allies might well escalate, and both sides might behave more like blocs competing for economic and financial preponderance than like partners submitting to the same rules of fair competition, free trade and monetary cooperation. This would be the case especially if the Community progresses far beyond the present stage of the EMS and begins to pool its foreign exchange reserves, to oversee the creation of national money and to use the ECU more widely.

The other external uncertainty is precisely the one that concerns the role of Europe on the world's diplomatic and strategic stage. The cold war has dominated that stage and the United States has felt strong enough to maintain its forces in Europe, its nuclear guarantee and the structure of NATO. In this situation, the different strategic priorities of France and West Germany, the different weapon systems of the British and French nuclear forces, the different assessments of the Soviet threat and of the perils and benefits of arms control among European countries, the institutional split between those that are part of the military organization of NATO and France, which insists on its autonomy-all condemned the European undertaking to remaining what is sometimes called a mere civilian power, or a merchants' enterprise.

If the cold war continues to fade and the United States shifts its priorities to other issues and other continents, the West Europeans-still too close to the Red Army for comfort, but less dependent on American presence and protection against a clearly more defensive Soviet Union whose own priority had shifted to internal reform-would find it easier to build, over time, a common defense scheme with joint weapons procurement, a respectable conventional army (largely West German), a Franco-British nuclear shield and a predominantly deterrent strategy. We have not reached that stage yet; at present the negotiations on conventional force reductions are a NATO affair, and the West Germans are eager for military cuts, economic cooperation with the Warsaw Pact countries and political détente-rather than for a new West European security system. But the moment might arrive later, after conventional reductions have begun and the presence of both superpowers in Europe has shrunk.

In the more relaxed international climate of recent months, an economically powerful European Community has already begun to exert strong attraction on the countries of Eastern Europe, and to help the gradual transformation of two former Soviet satellites, Poland and Hungary, into states whose relation to Moscow would be comparable to Finland's. The new role of the Community in coordinating assistance-even from the United States-for Poland and Hungary was recognized by the leaders of the seven major industrialized nations in Paris on July 15. In the past, when the cold war heated up, the Federal Republic's allegiances to NATO and to Europe increasingly conflicted with the desire, not for German reunification, but for a rapprochement between the two Germanys, even though the Western orientation always prevailed. In a climate of détente, the two directions become far less divergent, and a strongly European Germany can have more influence on its neighbors to the East.

Thus, in the diplomatic and strategic realm, much depends on the fate of Gorbachev and on American policy toward him; here, unlike in the economic realm, Europe is not a full-fledged actor yet, and whether it becomes one will be settled by those very outside forces that have, since the Second World War, divided the old continent and dominated their respective halves.

The will to build a European entity, spurred by the ineffectiveness of purely national solutions, exists without a doubt in the economic domain, but the devaluation of the nation-state does not mean its demise, even in this area. In the traditional domain of power politics, paradoxically, the progress of European unity depends on the devaluation of power politics-something that has often been prophesied, but has never in the past lasted for very long. Will the logic of economic efficiency and the fear of modern war combine to make the future radically different from the past?

The answer will depend, in part, on the lifting of a last uncertainty, which is both internal and external, and which could affect the Community even-indeed especially-if the future is different and if the fears of military insecurity in Western Europe diminish. It concerns West Germany.

There can be no European Community without Bonn and Paris. In Paris a new generation of politicians and high civil servants appears to have come to the conclusion that France's national objectives-except, perhaps, in the realm of nuclear weapons-can only be reached through European means. But some Europeans fear that the Federal Republic, now the dominant economy in Western Europe and (largely thanks to this) the central player in East-West relations in Europe, might in coming years reach exactly the opposite conclusion. They fear that Bonn might find excessive the burdens imposed by the Community (for instance, German contributions to the costly Common Agricultural Policy and to the structural funds that subsidize the poorer members), that Bonn might decide that West German industry is sufficiently strong, and that West German interests in Eastern Europe are sufficiently distinctive and important to make further ties between Bonn and the other Community members unnecessary, rendering obsolete the function of legitimation that the Community provided when Bonn was weak and widely distrusted.

Until now, in truth, the balance of benefits and burdens imposed by the Community on West Germany has been very favorable (e.g., West German farmers are admirably protected by the Community). While the recent behavior of West German officials and businessmen (such as Foreign Minister Hans-Dietrich Genscher's enthusiasm for Gorbachev, Kohl's about-face on the taxation of interest, and West German refusal to buy the superior French technology for fast railways) and the prospect of a Socialist-Green coalition government in the future have awakened such fears in France, the nightmare of Bonn's emancipation from its Western orientation appears unwarranted. However, the need to provide West Germany with sufficient benefits to keep this orientation worthwhile may itself create tensions in other countries (for example France, whose population is growing faster than Germany's, may want greater possibilities of economic growth than the Deutschmark-dominated EMS allows). Will France and others be willing to tolerate West German hegemony in the Community under any circumstances or in every field?

Such a predicament might well never occur, however. Each of the major West European players might continue to display enough of a mix of strengths and weaknesses to rule out the preponderance of any one of them. In the near future the Community is likely to keep progressing, although more laboriously as the tougher issues, long postponed, have to be faced; it is also likely to serve at least as a common shelter against an eventual recession, unlike in the 1970s. Ultimately, as in the 1950s and 1960s, the European Community's capacity to unite and its limits will be shaped by the events in, and the moves of, the other major countries of the world at least as much as by the patchwork of ties established among the interest groups, the parties and the people and by the domestic politics and economic performances of its member nations.

Stanley Hoffmann is Douglas Dillon Professor of The Civilization of France and Chairman of the Center for European Studies at Harvard University.

Britain in the New Europe

GEOFFREY SMITH

Winston Churchill

One of John Major's early remarks when he became prime minister in November 1990 was that he wanted Britain to be at the heart of Europe. It says something for the often fractious nature of Britain's relations with its European Community partners that this was regarded as a novel, even a controversial, statement. The comment was taken to be an implied criticism of his predecessor, Margaret Thatcher, whose dealings with other EC leaders had been more distant when they were not positively stormy

It has been a beneficial change of tone. The new approach enabled Major to win some concessions from his fellow heads of government in negotiating the Maastricht Treaty on European Union last December—in particular, the right to opt out of the social chapter and to decide later whether to join a single European currency. It has equipped him to play a pivotal role now in the most serious internal crisis that the EC has faced for at least a quarter century.

When Danish voters rejected the Maastricht Treaty in a referendum at the beginning of June they presented the Community with both a legal dilemma and a moral challenge. The Maastricht agreement provides for a number of amendments to the EC'S original Treaty of Rome, all of which require the unanimous endorsement of the 12 member states. If the Danes cannot be persuaded to change their minds, Maastricht in its present form is dead.

To get around this legal roadblock there have been some ominous rumblings that Denmark might be pressed to withdraw from the Community. Or, it has been suggested, the other 11 countries might sign another agreement, quite separate from the Treaty of Rome, to implement Maastricht. Neither stratagem would be a satisfactory solution to the dilemma.

Because the legal position has become so messy, people throughout the EC have begun to think more carefully about what sort of Europe they want. Before the Danes voted, nobody doubted that Maastricht would be ratified. Britain was the only other country until then where there had been a serious debate on the treaty's implications. Now the critics are raising their voices in a number of member states. The wisdom of Maastricht can no longer be assumed. Hearts and minds have to be won for the treaty, or something different must be found.

There is also the problem of Yugoslavia. Throughout the era of Soviet domination of eastern Europe, the ethnic, national and religious rivalries that have plagued the region for centuries were kept firmly under control. Once that grip was removed there was always the danger that these ancient feuds would resurface. That they should do so first in Yugoslavia is ironic because this was a country that escaped from Stalin's grasp nearly fifty years ago. But what has been happening there is symbolic both of the perils that lurk throughout eastern Europe and of the challenge they present for western Europe. The EC bears no responsibility for the onset of the catastrophe unfolding on Europe's rim. But because the Community appears so powerful, it is expected to find an answer to that crisis on its periphery.

It falls to John Major to play the principal part in attempting to steer the Community through these dangerous waters. For the second half of this year it is Britain's turn to be president of the Council; the British prime minister has a double responsibility. He has the chairman's duty to seek harmony, to guide all the members around the legal and political rocks: there must be no shipwreck on his watch. But he is also the heir to a distinctive British approach to the future of Europe.

II

The sharp difference of Major's style and tactics have obscured the similarity in the substance of the Major and Thatcher European policies. The harshness of Thatcher's rhetoric made it appear that she differed from her predecessors more than she really did. There certainly has not been consistency in the British attitude toward Europe over the past half century. But there have been certain fundamental themes that have kept reappearing, clothed at different times in different detailed policies, since Winston Churchill first sparked the imagination with his call upon a devastated Europe to unite.

Churchill began to alert public opinion to the problems of postwar Europe well before the end of World War II was in sight. He had in mind a Council of Europe that would operate under the United Nations "with all the strongest forces concerned woven into its texture, with a High Court to adjust disputes and with forces, armed forces, national or international or both, held ready to impose these decisions." He was evidently thinking in rather generalized terms of an elaborate exercise in regional peacekeeping.

Then, after he was thrown out of office in 1945, there came the loud trumpet blasts for the cause of a united Europe in a series of speeches, first in Zurich in 1946, then in London the following year when launching the United Europe Movement and finally at The Hague in 1948. The scorching, compelling power of Churchill's rhetoric had a dramatic impact on governments and peoples throughout Western Europe. The Council of Europe was established at his instigation in 1949 as an assembly for dialogue among parliamentarians. The process of developing European unity had begun. Never since then has Britain been so clearly at the heart of Europe.

Yet for all their inspirational qualities Churchill's speeches on Europe shared one characteristic with the plays of Shakespeare: it is possible to find in them a text for all seasons. On Europe Churchill used words expansively to convey a sentiment without too much regard for their precise meaning. Not infrequently, for example, he referred to his aspiration for "a United States of Europe." This phrase is used today to point toward a tightly integrated Community, based upon the example of the most powerful nation state in the world. Yet that was not what Churchill had in mind; on other occasions he displayed suspicion of supranational institutions.

Churchill seemed uncharacteristically relaxed in his choice of words on Europe because he was concerned above all to engender a spirit rather than to construct a system. His principal objective was to bring about an ethos of reconciliation, especially between France and Germany. "There must be an end to retribution," he proclaimed during his 1946 speech at Zurich University. "The first step in the recreation of the European family must be a partnership between France and Germany."

Churchill did not specify how this partnership should be formed. Time and again he warned against detailed plans and blueprints. "It would not be wise in this critical time," he declared at The Hague, "to be drawn into labored attempts to draw rigid structures of constitutions." In this he provided a direct contrast to Jean Monnet, the French businessman and administrator who was the godfather of the European Community.

Monnet believed just as deeply in reconciliation between the wartime foes, but his method was to create supranational economic institutions for a political purpose. Locking European economies together in this way would serve a double purpose: another war between Germany and France would become impossible, and Western Europe would become once more a power in the world.

This difference between the pragmatic Englishman and the programmatic Frenchman illustrates a fundamental difference in approach that has bedeviled relations between Britain and its partners. For those of the Monnet school, which has included most member governments for most of the time, the establishment of new structures for ever closer integration is an end in itself. This is what building the new Europe is all about: welding the nation states of the old Europe into a new economic and political entity.

Churchill offered a different vision. It was of a Europe moving toward closer economic, military and political unity, but with the precise arrangements to be determined by the flow of history. It was not to be a narrow, restricted Europe. "We aim at the eventual participation," he declared at The Hague, "of all European peoples whose society and way of life, making all allowances for the different points of view in various countries, are not in disaccord with a Charter of Human Rights and with the sincere expression of free democracy." Nor was it to be an exclusive or inward-looking Europe. "We in Britain must move in harmony with our great partners in the Commonwealth," he said in that same speech. Equally, he would have been the last person to suggest that Britain should modify its relationship with the United States in order to devote itself to Europe.

This strategy—broad, relaxed and generous—provided scope for flexibility, but also for misunderstanding. In 1950, while the British Conservatives under Churchill were still in opposition, two far-reaching European initiatives were launched. Robert Schuman, the French foreign minister, proposed the pooling of coal and steel production. René Pleven, the French prime minister, presented a plan for a European army.

The European Coal and Steel Community (ECSC), comprising France, West Germany, Italy, Belgium, the Netherlands and Luxembourg, became the first step in the process of European economic integration. There could have been no more dramatic beginning than to merge the two basic industries which were essential for conducting war. The scheme for a European Defence Community (EDC) was rejected by the French National Assembly in 1954, but it had dominated the European debate in the early 1950s.

The British Labour government did not join either project. It declined an invitation to take part in initial exploratory discussions on the ECSC with France and Germany because of a difference that may seem trivial but was symptomatic of a much deeper divergence. The French government wanted acceptance of the plan in principle before the details were worked out. The British refused to commit themselves without knowing what the full project would entail.

III

It was the kind of disagreement that has emerged time and again in subsequent years. The French in particular, but Britain's other European partners as well, want the reassurance of knowing that their companions have signed up for the whole voyage. This shows that everyone is together in spirit, even if there may be difficulties along the way.

The British, by contrast, are mistrustful of windy general declarations. They take promises more literally, so they want to be careful what they are signing. It is no accident that Britain has caused more difficulty than anyone else over the years about accepting what seem to their partners to be innocuous statements of intent while, on the other hand, having one of the best records in implementing EC legislation once it has been passed in Brussels.

Churchill criticized the Labour government for failing to take part in the preparatory talks, saying that Britain could have claimed the right to withdraw later if it did not like the outcome. On the European army he was even more positive, telling the Council of Europe that "we should make a gesture of practical and constructive guidance by declaring ourselves in favor of the immediate creation of a European army under a unified command, and in which we should bear a worthy and honorable part."

Yet when Churchill became prime minister again in 1951 Britain did not join either project. Britain's exclusion from the process of European integration could no longer be attributed simply to having a Labour government. Thereafter Britain was clearly on the periphery, politically as well as geographically. To some of Churchill's own supporters and to many in other European countries it came as a grave disappointment, almost a betrayal, that the great champion of European unity in opposition was not prepared to take action when he was back in office.

Was it, as Harold Macmillan implied in his memoirs, that Churchill just had other things on his mind? That was no doubt part of it. He had resumed the leadership of a country in grave economic difficulties, and he was preoccupied with the threat of nuclear warfare. His foreign secretary, Anthony Eden, and the Foreign Office at that time did not share his European enthusiasm. They would not have prompted Churchill to remember his earlier words, and he might have hesitated to push them in a direction where he knew they did not want to go.

But there were other reasons as well. Churchill had never committed himself to a precise scheme in either case, and he did not like the way in which the original ideas had been developed. In his June 1950 speech to the House of Commons, criticizing the British government for failing to take part in the original negotiations on the ECSC, he had criticized the French for making precise stipulations before being ready to discuss, and he had commented sourly on "the usual jargon about 'the infrastructure of a supranational authority'." That was not how he wanted Europe to develop.

This was why he did not take Britain into the EDC. It was not just a lapse of memory, as he explained to the House of Commons in July 1954:

I am sometimes reproached with having led France to expect that Britain would be a full member of the European Defence Community. When in 1950 I proposed at Strasbourg the creation of a European army, I had in mind—and it is clear from my speech—the formation of a long-term grand alliance under which national armies would operate under a unified allied command. The policy of the alliance would, I assumed, be decided jointly by the governments of the participating countries. My conception involved no supranational institutions, and I saw no difficulty in Britain playing a full part in a scheme of that kind. However, the French approached this question from a constitutional, rather than a purely military, point of view. The result was that when they and the other five continental nations worked out a detailed scheme, it took the form of a complete merger of national forces under federal supranational control.

So by the mid-1950s a gulf had developed between even the pro-Europeans in Britain and the core movement for European unity. The same six countries that had formed the ECSC and that had tried and failed to set up the EDC were shortly to create the Common Market. In each case there was to be a supranational operating arm subject to the control of a council of ministers from the member governments.

In Britain there were many, far more than there are today, who were either hostile or at best tepid toward the whole idea of European entanglements in peacetime. But even those who were genuinely enthusiastic were often opposed to the supranational preferences of the Six. Many Britons wanted Europe to bury the old animosities, to play a more effective role in NATO, to recover its economic strength and to cooperate politically. But they were not seeking to create a new economic, political or military power in Western Europe. They were prepared to give up some national sovereignty, but only to the extent required for specific practical purposes. To most Britons the merging of sovereignty was not an end in itself.

It was quite consistent with this attitude that, after the collapse of the EDC, Britain should then play the leading role in the creation of the Western European Union (WEU) in 1955. One of the purposes of the EDC had been to provide a framework within which West Germany could be rearmed and brought into NATO without causing alarm to its neighbors. It was now agreed that Britain should join the Six in founding this new defense grouping with a promise to keep significant military forces on the continent. This was an unequivocal British commitment to Europe for a practical purpose, but without the supranational trappings to which Churchill and others had so objected.

The contrast between the failure of the EDC, for which Britain was widely blamed, and the successful negotiation of WEU illustrated the fundamental difference in attitude between Britain and the Six. It was not altogether surprising, therefore, that Britain was not represented when the Six met at the Sicilian town of Messina in 1955 to plan a customs union. Britain did send someone to sit on the preparatory committee that followed the Messina conference, but only a civil servant from the Board of Trade, not a person with the political clout of the other representatives.

The British delegation was in an invidious position, outranked around the conference table and unsupported from home. It had difficulty obtaining instructions from London, so it could hardly have played much of a part in the discussions. By then Anthony Eden, the unenthusiastic European, had succeeded Churchill. Macmillan, who had become foreign secretary, had been one of the most ardent of British Europeans in the postwar years. He would have had difficulty in overcoming Eden's skepticism, but Macmillan himself was not enamored of the supranationalism that was evident once again in the proposed structure of the EC. In any case the general feeling in London was that nothing would come of this latest venture in European integration.

When this nonchalance proved to be unfounded, and the Six proceeded to sign the Treaty of Rome that created the Common Market in March 1957, British casualness turned to consternation. The mirage had become a threat. It was to counter the danger of exclusion from this new, powerful economic grouping that Britain now put forward a scheme for an industrial free trade area encompassing the whole of Western Europe, with the EC joining as a single unit.

After tortuous negotiations that proceeded for nearly two years the French government killed the project in November 1958, a few months after de Gaulle's return to power. Yet, though the idea was stillborn, the plan indicated some of the enduring British preferences. The unifying process should be extended as widely as possible across Europe, not confined to a small group of the rich and powerful. Free trade is the economic goal that matters most; the concentration of power at the center is at best a necessary evil. (There would have been no supranational authority for the free trade area itself.)

When this scheme was rejected, the next option was to negotiate the European Free Trade Association (EFTA) with the Scandinavian countries, Austria, Switzerland and Portugal. This 1960 agreement was essentially a gathering of the outsiders. While it served to increase trade substantially among its members, Britain soon concluded that such an arrangement could be no more than second best.

The historic decision to apply for full EC membership came in the summer of 1961. There had been no mention of a possible application in the party manifesto when the Conservatives won the general election of 1959, merely a reference to EFTA and the continued aspiration for industrial free trade throughout Western Europe. But after long agonizing, the government decided that if Britain remained outside the Community it would be on the sidelines of European development.

In presenting the British case to the EC governments in Paris in October that year Edward Heath, the minister responsible for the negotiations, put it in terms of a historic conversion. Two months earlier Prime Minister Macmillan had been a little more circumspect in the House of Commons. He had put the emphasis very much upon the economic advantages of being part of a larger market: "The Treaty of Rome does not deal with defense. It does not deal with foreign policy." It was a strange irony that Macmillan should have referred specifically to these two fields of policy, because the Community's incursion into these areas is one of the causes of controversy today. He then spoke more explicitly about the kind of Community into which he hoped to lead the British people:

I fully accept that there are some forces in Europe which would like a genuine federalist solution. ... They would like Europe to turn itself into a sort of United States, but I believe this to be a completely false analogy.... . Europe is too old, too diverse in tradition, language and history to find itself united by such means.... . The alternative concept, the only practical concept, would be a confederation, a commonwealth, if honorable members would like to call it that—what I think General de Gaulle has called Europe des patries—which would retain the great traditions and the pride of individual nations while working together in clearly defined spheres for their common interest.

It is revealing that he should have used the words Europe des patries. The phrase is associated today with those who want a watered-down version of the Community— Euroskeptics lacking a true vision of Europe. Yet this was the concept of the Community given to the British people by the prime minister who first tried to take the country in.

Macmillan was not lacking in European enthusiasm. He probably had been Churchill's closest colleague in the heady days of the early European conferences at The Hague and Strasbourg. It is just that right from the beginning there have been competing philosophies of the direction that European unity should take. But Macmillan was thwarted in his endeavor by the man whose phrase he borrowed. At a notorious press conference in Paris on January 14, 1963, de Gaulle made it clear that France would veto Britain's application. His objections were fundamental. Britain was too insular, a maritime power, "linked through her exchanges, her markets, her supply lines to the most diverse and often the most distant countries."

The French leader was not referring here only to Britain's Commonwealth connections. He was known to be particularly disturbed by the fear that Britain was too close to the United States, that Britain would be an American Trojan horse inside the EC—a suspicion that a number of Britain's partners still retain.

It was to be almost another decade before Britain was able to join. Edward Heath, who was by then prime minister, was the most fervent European to lead any British government of either party. Nonetheless he had to be careful. The public opinion polls in the early 1970s suggested that most British people were opposed to membership.

Heath showed considerable diplomatic skill in the way that he maneuvered Britain into EC membership. Recognizing that there was no way to bypass a French veto, he managed to persuade de Gaulle's successor, Georges Pompidou, of Britain's European convictions. Yet he could not afford to sound any clarion call at home, for fear of provoking public opinion. The Conservative manifesto at the election of June 1970, which preceded the opening of negotiations, proclaimed with studied caution: "Our sole commitment is to negotiate; no more, no less."

So before Britain went into the Community in January 1973, the question was not an issue at a general election. Nor was there a referendum on it. There was no dramatic public debate. Heath made the reasonable but low-key pitch that the EC was too important to stay out of, and he made much of the economic benefits of membership. He certainly drew attention to the political considerations, but the British people were not given to understand that they would be embarking on the construction of a European superstate.

Paradoxically it was only after the defeat of the Heath government that British membership ceased to be controversial at home. The Labour government that came to power in March 1974 was, as so often, badly divided on Europe. Seven years earlier the then Labour prime minister, Harold Wilson, and his foreign secretary, George Brown, had traveled around the capitals of the Six in the attempt to have the French veto lifted, proclaiming that they would not take no for an answer. They had no choice.

When the Heath government had managed to take Britain in, the Labour Party was severely split, with most of its members of parliament voting against. Back in office most members of the Cabinet wanted to keep Britain in the Community, but they needed a pretext to cover their inconsistency and some device to prevent the party tearing itself apart. So there was an essentially cosmetic exercise in renegotiating the terms of British entry, and the new arrangements were put to a referendum of the British electorate.

The result was a majority of nearly two to one in favor of staying in. From that day on, the question of British membership has never been in serious contention. But the nature of the Community in which Britain has found a home has been and remains in dispute.

IV

The issue was dramatized during Margaret Thatcher's years in power by the pugnacious style in which she conducted her arguments with other EC leaders. There were tempestuous debates on Britain's contribution to the Community budget, on the Common Agricultural Policy, on trade policy and on many other issues.

Her instincts were never those of a European. Her emotional rapport was with the United States, especially during the Reagan presidency. But while in her heart she might not have been too sorry to see Britain leave the Community, that has never been her policy. Her rhetoric may have encouraged the isolationists in Britain, but her world view never stopped at the English Channel. Her difficulty with the EC was that her horizons extended far beyond Europe.

In their very different ways she and John Major have been pursuing similar fundamental objectives, the themes that have been evident in the British approach to Europe over the past half century.

First, the EC should be as decentralized as possible. From the early days of the movement for European unity there has been a powerful school of thought whose primary purpose has been to build Europe into a power in its own right. This Europe was to be a bulwark against the Soviet Union at the worst of the Cold War; then, as the Cold War became less intense, it would be a distinctive voice between the Soviet Union and the United States; and now the Maastricht agreement is to make Europe strong enough to compete economically with the United States and Japan. Those who want to build Europe into a major power must wish it to develop into a tightly integrated unit, economically, politically and militarily. The mechanism becomes its own objective.

The British have always had a more modest conception of Europe. The purpose of European unity in their eyes has been to enable the peoples of Europe to live more harmoniously together and to enjoy greater prosperity and influence. Any measure of centralization needs to be justified on pragmatic grounds. For some years this attitude combined with traditional British insularity to keep Britain out of the ECSC and then the Common Market. Now it makes the British suspicious of the authority of Brussels—yet not totally hostile, it must be added, where a specific benefit can be seen.

In 1985 Margaret Thatcher agreed to an increase in majority voting in the Council of Ministers—which must expand the danger of any country having policies imposed upon it against its will—as part of the Single European Act. That legislation provided for the 1992 program, introducing the Single European Market with the elimination of trade barriers between all members of the Community. This is an enlargement of free trade, which Thatcher much approves of, and she was persuaded that more majority voting was required if the program was not going to be blocked by one country or another.

Other integrationist measures will be acceptable with a similar pragmatic justification. In general, though, there is a widespread British belief that there is too much interference from Brussels. The intense debate over the Maastricht Treaty revolves around this issue. The question in Britain today is not whether a decentralized Community is desirable, but whether Maastricht provides for that decentralization.

John Major has claimed that "the Maastricht Treaty marks the point at which, for the first time, we have begun to reverse that centralizing trend. We have moved decision-taking back towards the member states in areas where Community law need not and should not apply." He had in mind two of the decisions at Maastricht: that foreign and security policies, justice and immigration should be matters for intergovernmental cooperation outside the normal processes of the Community; and that in such areas as the environment, health, education and social policy the Community should act only if the objective cannot be achieved by the member states.

This is the principle of "subsidiarity" about which so much is heard throughout the EC these days. Major's critics are deeply skeptical as to whether it will be implemented, and they point to the extension of the Community's power to act in other fields. They believe that the treaty would inevitably impose more integration. But Major is seeking to interpret it, perhaps to reinterpret it, so as to move the EC in the opposite direction. The significance of this dispute is that both sides are claiming to be the better decentralizers.

V

Another consistent British theme has been that Europe should be organized on the basis of competition and free trade. This does not mean free trade just among the existing 12 members. It is one of the reasons why Britain is more eager than others to bring a number of new applicants into the Community as quickly as possible.

It is sometimes alleged that the cause of enlargement is pressed particularly hard by those who believe that it will prevent the EC from becoming too tightly integrated. There is some truth in this. In the long run the larger the Community, the more flexibility will have to be allowed. But the campaign for enlargement is more than a convenient tactical ploy.

There is a direct line of descent from Churchill's desire to encompass the whole of Europe, to Macmillan's fear of splitting Western Europe when the Common Market was founded, to Thatcher's 1988 remark in her controversial Bruges speech that "We must never forget that east of the Iron Curtain peoples who once enjoyed a full share of European culture, freedom and identity have been cut off from their roots. We shall always look on Warsaw, Prague and Budapest as great European cities." Churchill spoke before the Common Market was contemplated, and Thatcher a year before the Berlin Wall came down and therefore before there was any possibility of any of the former Warsaw Pact countries becoming members.

Since then both Thatcher and Major have spoken of the possibility of the EC extending one day even to Russia. As with Churchill in earlier years such remarks should be taken not as specific proposals but as evidence of an attitude. Britain does not want a narrow Community.

When Britain first contemplated joining the Common Market, the question was how it could combine membership with its role in the Commonwealth. Then there came the tension between Britain's place in Europe and its relationship with the United States. Britain's view of its place in the world has changed over the years. It is becoming more European. More people travel there, work there and do business there. Europe matters far more than it did and the Commonwealth far less.

The relationship with the United States still matters. Whether it matters as much as Britain's European connection is immaterial. The British interest lies in not having to choose. The new Europe that Britain needs is one where the member states can be European without being false to their history.

The search for Britain's kind of Europe is in some ways more realistic and more relevant now than in the early days of the European movement when Churchill and his friends were in the vanguard, trying to reconcile France and Germany and to build up the strength of Western Europe.

Today the greatest threat to stability in western Europe lies in the threat of disorder in eastern Europe. The former Yugoslavia, with its growing death count and suffering, is a symptom of what could occur elsewhere in eastern Europe, which might in turn undermine security in the West.

To British eyes it is a matter of self-interest to extend a hand to the fledgling democracies to the east. Yet there is a paradox here. In the Gulf War Britain was one of those most ready to use force and was, indeed, palpably disappointed by the caution of most of its European partners. Now Britain is one of those most reluctant to become militarily engaged in Yugoslavia.

The apparent contradiction comes from a difference in strategic appreciation. The British view is that force can be justified (apart from cases of straightforward self-defense) in pursuit of specific objectives that can be achieved in a limited period of time. Those conditions applied in the gulf and in the Falklands.

In the case of Yugoslavia there is fear of being bogged down in a conflict that can be neither won nor lost, while being shot at from both sides. Therefore the British have placed the emphasis on negotiation as the prerequisite for peace. Whether this is a wise judgment or not, it does not indicate any lack of concern about eastern Europe.

VI

Just as Britain wants an open and expanding Community in Europe, it no less wishes to avoid presenting a Fortress Europe to the rest of the world. It was John Major at Maastricht who insisted that industrial policy must still be settled by unanimous agreement among all member governments, thereby reducing the risk of a protectionist policy being foisted on the Community. It was Major again who tried, unavailingly this time, at the Munich summit of the Group of Seven leading industrial nations in July to persuade his Community partners to accept a further reduction in European agricultural subsidies, and so remove the obstacle in the way of the Uruguay Round of the General Agreement on Tariffs and Trade.

It is easier, however, for Britain to take this enlightened view because it has a much lower proportion of its work force in agriculture than either France or Germany. It would also stand to suffer particularly badly from any international trade war. Although Britain has shifted its pattern of trade much more to the Community, it still sells a higher proportion of its exports outside Europe than any other member.

The risks of a Fortress Europe now seem to have receded. But protectionist pressures remain, and the devil lies in the details: in the implementation of anti-dumping legislation, for example, and in laying down standards for goods. Agreement on the Uruguay Round would be a critical advance, but any chance of a French compromise will have to wait until after their Maastricht referendum on September 20.

French rejection of the treaty via referendum (its National Assembly has already voted in favor of the treaty) would mark a critical turning point for the Community. No other country is still planning to hold a referendum (the Irish have already had theirs and voted in favor), but doubts about the treaty are much in evidence elsewhere. In Germany there is strong resistance to giving up the Deutsche mark later this decade for a new European Community currency. In Britain the government will not find it easy to steer the ratification bill through its remaining stages in parliament.

Even if Maastricht is finally endorsed by all the member countries, the Danish vote has changed attitudes in many parts of the Community. The dangers of excessive centralization of the Community are being widely appreciated.

The present uncertainty gives John Major his opportunity. He is positioning himself so as to stand the best chance of guiding the EC in a more decentralized direction, irrespective of whether the treaty is passed or rejected. He proclaims himself the unflinching friend of Maastricht, the loyal member of the EC who has been steady under fire in a critical position. If the treaty is ratified he will deserve a full share of the credit. If it fails he cannot be blamed by his fellow European leaders (yet they will know that he will find it easy, even congenial, to take an alternative course). In either event he should have a reasonable claim to their trust and attention.

Where Thatcher sought to resist the EC, Major is seeking to remold it, quietly and unostentatiously, into a Community in which Britain can feel more comfortable. It is a delicate maneuver, and he may fail. He may find that he has accepted more centralization than he realizes. He may offend both sides: upsetting his supporters at home by appearing to love Maastricht too much, and angering the more zealous European enthusiasts by being too keen on decentralization. But he is a master of the political smokescreen. At the moment that is both his greatest strength and presents his greatest danger.

Geoffrey Smith, a former columnist for The Times of London, is author of Reagan and Thatcher.

Europe's Endangered Liberal Order

Timothy Garton Ash

The flags of Berlin, Germany and the European Union blow in the wind near the conference center for the upcoming European Union summit of the European leaders in Berlin on March 23, 1999.

THE DREAM IS HERE

Like no other continent, Europe is obsessed with its own meaning and direction. Idealistic and teleological visions of Europe at once inform, legitimate, and are themselves informed and legitimated by the political development of something now called the European Union. The name "European Union" is itself a product of this approach, for a union is what the EU is meant to be, not what it is.

European history since 1945 is told as a story of unification: difficult, delayed, suffering reverses, but nonetheless progressing. This is the grand narrative taught to millions of European schoolchildren and accepted by central and east European politicians when they speak of rejoining "a uniting Europe." That narrative's next chapter is even now being written by a leading German historian, Dr. Helmut Kohl. Its millennial culmination is to be achieved on January 1, 1999, with a monetary union that will, it is argued, irreversibly bind together some of the leading states of Europe. This group of states should in turn become the "magnetic core" of a larger unification.

European unification is presented not just as a product of visionary leaders from Jean Monnet and Robert Schuman to Francois Mitterrand and Helmut Kohl but also as a necessary, even an inevitable response to the contemporary forces of globalization. Nation-states are no longer able to protect and realize their economic and political interests on their own. They are no match for transnational actors like global currency speculators, multinational companies, or international criminal gangs. Both power and identity, it is argued, are migrating upward and downward from the nation-state: upward to the supranational level, downward to the regional one. In a globalized world of large trading blocs, Europe will only be able to hold its own as a larger political-economic unit. Thus Manfred Rommel, the popular former mayor of Stuttgart, declares, "We live under the dictatorship of the global economy. There is no alternative to a united Europe."

It would be absurd to suggest that there is no substance to these claims. Yet when combined into a single grand narrative, into the idealistic-teleological discourse of European unification, they result in a dangerously misleading picture of the real ground on which European leaders will have to build at the beginning of the twenty-first century. In fact, what we have already achieved in a large part of western and southern Europe is a new model of liberal order. But this extraordinary achievement is itself now under threat precisely as a result of the forced march to unity. What we should be doing now is rather to consolidate this liberal order and to spread it across the continent. Liberal order, not unity, is the right strategic goal for European policy in our time.

THE PAST AS WARNING

In the index to Arnold Toynbee's A Study of History, we find "Europe, as battlefield," "Europe, as not an intelligible field of historical study," and, finally, "Europe, unification of, failure of attempts at." Toynbee is an unreliable source, but he raises important questions about the long sweep of European history. The most fundamental point is his second one. Is the thing to be united actually a cultural-historical unit? If so, where does it begin and end? It is, Toynbee claims, a "cultural misapplication of a nautical term" to suggest that the Mediterranean ancient history of Greece and Rome and modern Western history are successive acts in a single European drama. He prefers the Polish historian Oskar Halecki's account, in which a Mediterranean age is followed by a European age, running roughly from 950 to 1950, which in turn is succeeded by what Halecki called an Atlantic age. Today we might refer to our era simply as a global age.

Yet even in the European age, the continent's eastern edge remained deeply ill-defined. Was it the Elbe? Or the dividing line between western and eastern Christianity? Or the Urals? Europe's political history was characterized by the astounding diversity of peoples, nations, states, and empires and by the ceaseless and often violent competition between them. In short, no continent was externally more ill-defined, internally more diverse, or historically more disorderly. Yet no continent produced more schemes for its own orderly unification. So our teleological-idealistic or Whig interpreters can cite an impressive list of intellectual and political forebears, from the Bohemian King George of Podebrady through the Duc de Sully and William Penn (writing already in America) to Aristide Briand and Richard Coudenhove-Kalergi, the prophet of Pan-Europa. The trouble is that those designs for European unification that were peaceful were not implemented, while those that were implemented were not peaceful. The reality of unification was either a temporary solidarity in response to an external invader or an attempt by one European state to establish continental hegemony by force of arms, from Napoleon to Hitler. But the latter also failed, as Toynbee's index dryly notes.

The attempt at European unification since 1945 thus stands out from all earlier attempts by being both peaceful and partially implemented. An idealistic interpretation of this historical abnormality is that we Europeans have at last learned from history. The "European civil war" of 1914 to 1945, that second and still bloodier Thirty Years' War, finally brought us to our senses. Yet this requires a little closer examination. For only after the end of the Cold War are we discovering just how much European integration owed to it. First, there was the Soviet Union as negative external integrator. West Europeans pulled together in the face of the common enemy, as they had before the Mongols or the Turks. Second, there was the United States as positive external integrator. Particularly in the earlier years, the United States pushed very strongly for West European integration, making it almost a condition for further Marshall Plan aid. In later decades, the United States was at times more ambivalent about building up a rival trading bloc, but in broad geopolitical terms it supported West European integration throughout the Cold War.

Third, the Cold War helped, quite brutally, by cutting off most of central and eastern Europe behind the Iron Curtain. This meant that European integration could begin between a relatively small number of bourgeois democracies at roughly comparable economic levels and with important older elements of common history. As has often been observed, the frontiers of the original European Economic Community of six were roughly coterminous with those of Charlemagne's Holy Roman Empire. The EEC was also centered around what historical geographers have called the "golden banana" of advanced European economic development, stretching from Manchester to Milan via the Low Countries, eastern France and western Germany. Moreover, within this corner of the continent there were important convergences or trade offs between the political and economic interests of the nations involved-the crucial ones being between France and Germany. None of this is to deny a genuine element of European idealism among the elites of that time. But the more we discover about this earlier period, the more hard-nosed and nationally self-interested the main actors appear. Contrary to the received view, the idealists are more to be found in the next generation: that of Helmut Kohl rather than Konrad Adenauer. There is no mistaking the genuine enthusiasm with which Kohl describes, as he will at the slightest prompting, the unforgettable experience of lifting the first frontier barriers between France and Germany, just a few years after the end of the war.

The national interests propelling closer intra-European ties were still powerfully present in the 1970s and 1980s. Britain, most obviously, joined the EEC in hopes of reviving its own flagging economy and buttressing its declining influence in the world. In a 1988 book entitled La France par l'Europe, none other than Jacques Delors wrote that "creating Europe is a way of regaining that room for manoeuvre necessary for 'a certain idea of France.'" (The phrase "a certain idea of France" was, of course, de Gaulle's.) In my book In Europe's Name I have shown how German enthusiasm for European integration was nourished by the need to secure wider European and American support for improved relations with the communist east and, eventually, the reunification of Germany. Finally, there was also a growing perception of real common European interests.

As a result of the confluence of these three kinds of motive and those three favorable external conditions, the 1970s and 1980s saw an impressive set of steps toward closer political cooperation and economic and legal integration. Starting with the Hague summit of December 1969, they included direct elections to the European Parliament, the founding of the European Monetary System, the Single European Act, and the great project of completing the internal market in the magic year of "1992."

This dynamic process, against a background of renewed economic growth and the spread of democracy to southern Europe, did contribute directly to the end of the Cold War. One of the reasons behind Mikhail Gorbachev's "new thinking" in foreign policy was Soviet alarm at the prospect of being left still further behind by a "Europe" that was seen as technologically advanced, economically dynamic, and rapidly integrating behind high protective walls. How much more was this true of the peoples of east central Europe, who anyway felt themselves to belong culturally and historically to Europe, felt this with the passion of the excluded-and for whom the prosperous Western Europe they saw on their travels now clearly represented the better alternative to a discredited and stagnant "real socialism." Accordingly, one of the great slogans of the velvet revolutions of 1989 was "the return to Europe." In this sense one could argue, in apparent defiance of chronology, that "1992" in Western Europe was one of the causes of 1989 in Eastern Europe. But the end of the Cold War also ended a historical constellation that was particularly favorable to a particular model of West European integration.

THE PRESENT AS CONFUSION

We cannot judge the period since 1989 in the same way, as history. The case is still being heard, and the evidence is contradictory. On the one hand, we have seen further incremental diminution in the effective powers and sovereignty of established nation-states inside the EU. The Maastricht program, with European monetary union as its central project, is supposed to make a further decisive step to unification by the end of the decade. Yet this decade has also seen the explosive emergence of at least a dozen new nation-states. Indeed, there are now more states on the map of Europe than ever before in the twentieth century. In the former Yugoslavia, these new states emerged through war, ethnic cleansing, and the violent redrawing of frontiers. In the former Czechoslovakia, the separation into two states was carried out peacefully, by negotiation. In the former Soviet Union, there were variations in between.

Nor is this phenomenon of de-unification confined to the postcommunist half of Europe. The cliché of "integration in the west, disintegration in the east" does not bear closer examination. It is surprising, for example, to see the progressive disintegration of Belgium cited as evidence of the decline of the nation-state and the rise of regionalism, for the tensions that are pulling Belgium apart would be entirely familiar to a nineteenth-century nationalist. Each ethnolinguistic group is demanding a growing measure of self-government. My own country, Britain, has for decades been an unusual modern variation on the theme of nation-state: a state composed of four nations-or, to be precise, three and a part. But now the constituent nations, especially Scotland, are pulling away toward a larger measure of self-government.

And what of Europe's central power? Since 1989 Germany has reemerged as a fully sovereign nation-state. In Berlin, we are witnessing the extraordinary architectural reconstruction of the grandiose capital of a historic nation-state. Yet at the same time, Germany's political leaders, above all Helmut Kohl, are pressing ahead with all their considerable might to surrender that vital component of national sovereignty-and, particularly in the contemporary German case, also of identity-which is the national currency. There is a startling contradiction between, so to speak, the architecture in Berlin and the rhetoric in Bonn. I do not think this contradiction can be resolved dialectically, even in the homeland of the dialectic. In fact, Germany today is in a political-psychological condition that can only be described as Faustian, with two souls in one breast. If in 1999 monetary union goes ahead and the German government moves to Berlin, then the country will wake up in its new bed on January 1, 2000, scratch its head, and ask itself, "Now, why did we just give up the deutsche mark?"

What would be the answer? Of course there are economic arguments for monetary union. But monetary union was conceived as an economic means to a political end. It is the continuation of the functionalist approach adopted by the French and German founding fathers of the EEC: political integration through economic integration. But there was a more specific political reason for the decision to make this the central goal of European integration in the 1990s. As so often before, the key lies in a compromise between French and German national interests. In 1990, there was at the very least an implicit linkage made between Mitterrand's reluctant support for German unification and Kohl's decisive push towards European monetary union. "The whole of Deutschland for Kohl, half the deutsche mark for Mitterrand," some wits put it. Leading German politicians will acknowledge privately that monetary union is the price paid for German unification.

Yet to some extent, this is a price that Kohl wants to pay. For he wants to see the newly united Germany bound firmly and, as he himself puts it, "irreversibly," into Europe. Even more than his hero Adenauer, he believes that it is dangerous for Germany, with its erratic history and critical size-"too big for Europe, too small for the world," as Henry Kissinger once pithily observed-to stand alone in the center of Europe, trying to juggle or balance the nine neighbors and many partners around it. So Dr. Kohl's ultimate, unspoken answer to the question, "Why did we just give up the deutsche mark?" will be, "Because we Germans can't trust ourselves." To which a younger generation will say, "Why not?" Many of them see no reason why Germany needs to be bound to the mast like Odysseus to resist the siren calls of its awful past. They think Germany can be trusted to keep its own balance as a responsible, liberal nation-state inside an already close-knit community of other responsible, liberal nation-states. Certainly Kohl's implicit argument will not convince the man in the Bavarian beer tent. In opinion polls, a majority of Germans still do not want to give up the deutsche mark for the euro. So Germany, this newly restored nation-state, will enter monetary union full of reservations, doubts, and fears.

A HOUSE DIVIDED

Economists differ, and non-economists have to pick their way between the arguments. But few would dissent with the proposition that European monetary union (EMU) is an unprecedented, high-risk gamble. As several leading economists have pointed out, Europe lacks vital components that make monetary union work in the United States. The United States has high labor mobility, price and wage flexibility, provisions for automatic, large-scale budgetary transfers to states adversely affected by so-called asymmetric shocks, and, not least, the common language, culture, and shared history in a single country that make such transfers acceptable as a matter of course to citizens and taxpayers.

Europe has low labor mobility and high unemployment. It has relatively little wage flexibility. The EU redistributes a maximum of 1.27 percent of the GDP of its member states, and most of this is already committed to schemes such as the Common Agricultural Policy (cap) and the so-called structural funds for assisting poorer regions. It has no common language and certainly no common state. Since 1989, we have seen how reluctant West German taxpayers have been to pay even for their own compatriots in the east. Do we really expect that they would be willing to pay for the French unemployed as well? The Maastricht treaty does not provide for that, and leading German politicians have repeatedly stressed that they will not stand for it. The minimal trust and solidarity between citizens that is the fragile treasure of the democratic nation-state does not, alas, yet exist between the citizens of Europe. For there is no European demos-only a European telos.

Against this powerful critique, it is urged that the "asymmetric shocks" will affect different regions within European countries, and these countries do themselves make internal provision for automatic budgetary transfers. In France, it is also very optimistically suggested that reform of the cap and structural funds will free up EU resources for compensatory transfers between states. (But if we are serious about enlargement, some of these resources will also be needed for the much poorer new member states.) More economically liberal Europeans argue that monetary union will simply compel us to introduce more free-market flexibility, not least in wage levels. None of this makes a very persuasive rebuttal, especially since different European countries favor different kinds of response.

The dangers, by contrast, are all too obvious. EMU requires a single monetary policy and a single interest rate for all. What if that rate is right for Germany but wrong for Spain and Italy, or vice versa? And what if French unemployment continues to rise? As elections approach, national politicians will find the temptation to "blame it on EMU" almost irresistible. If responsible politicians resist the temptation, irresponsible ones will gain votes. And the European Central Bank will not start with any of the popular authority that the Bundesbank enjoys in Germany. It starts as the product of a political-bureaucratic procedure of "building Europe from above" that is even now-as the Maastricht referendum debate in France showed-perilously short of popular support and democratic legitimacy.

In fact, received wisdom in EU capitals is already that EMU will sooner or later face a crisis, perhaps after the end of a pre-millennium boom, in 2001 or 2002 (just as Britain is preparing to join). Euro-optimists hope this crisis will catalyze economic liberalization, European solidarity, and perhaps even those steps of political unification that historically have preceded, not followed, successful monetary unions. A shared fear of the catastrophic consequences of a failure of monetary union will draw Europeans together, as the shared fear of a common external enemy (Mongols, Turks, Soviets) did in the past. But it is a truly dialectical leap of faith to suggest that a crisis that exacerbates differences between European countries is the best way to unite them. The fact is that at Maastricht the leaders of the EU put the cart before the horse. Out of the familiar mixture of three different kinds of motive-idealistic, national-instrumental, and perceived common interest-they committed themselves to what was meant to be a decisive step to uniting Europe but now seems likely to divide even those who belong to the monetary union. At least in the short term, it will certainly divide those existing EU members who participate in the monetary union from those who do not: the so-called "ins" and "outs."

Meanwhile, the massive concentration on this single project has contributed to the neglect of the great opportunity that arose in the eastern half of the continent when the Berlin Wall came down. The Maastricht agenda of internal unification has taken the time and energy of West European leaders away from the agenda of eastward enlargement. To be sure, there is no theoretical contradiction between the "deepening" and the "widening" of the EU. Indeed, widening requires deepening. If the major institutions of the EU, originally designed to work for six member states, are still to function in a community of 26, then major reforms, necessarily involving a further sharing of sovereignty, are essential. But these changes are of a different kind from those required for monetary union. While there is no theoretical contradiction, there has been a practical tension between deepening and widening.

To put it plainly: our leaders set the wrong priority after 1989. We were like people who for 40 years had lived in a large, ramshackle house divided down the middle by a concrete wall. In the western half we had rebuilt, mended the roof, knocked several rooms together, redecorated, and installed new plumbing and electric wiring-while the eastern half fell into a state of dangerous decay. Then the wall came down. What did we do? We decided that what the whole house needed most urgently was a superb new computer-controlled system of air conditioning in the western half. While we prepared to install it, the eastern half of the house began to fall apart and catch fire. We fiddled in Maastricht while Sarajevo burned.

The best can so often be the enemy of the good. The rationalist, functionalist, perfectionist attempt to "make Europe" or "complete Europe" through a hard core built around a rapid monetary union could well end up achieving the opposite of the desired effect. One can all too plausibly argue that what we are likely to witness in the next five to ten years is the writing of another entry for Toynbee's index, under: "Europe, unification of, failure of attempts at." Some contemporary Cassandras go further still. They see the danger of us writing another entry under "Europe, as battlefield." One might answer that we already have, in the former Yugoslavia. But any suggestion that the forced march to unification through money brings the danger of violent conflict between West European states does seem overdrawn, for at least three reasons. First, there is the powerful neoKantian argument that bourgeois democracies are unlikely to go to war against each other. Second, unlike pre-1945 Europe, we have a generally benign extra-European hegemon in the United States. Third, to warn of violence is to ignore the huge and real achievement of European integration to date: the unique, unprecedented framework and deeply ingrained habits of permanent institutionalized cooperation that ensure that the conflicts of interest that exist-and will continue to exist-between the member states and nations are never resolved by force. All those endless hours and days of negotiation in Brussels between ministers from 15 European countries who end up knowing each other almost better than they know their own families: that is the essence of this Europe. It is an economic community, of course, but it is also a security community-a group of states that do find it unthinkable to resolve their own differences by war.

THE CASE FOR LIBERAL ORDER

Now one could certainly argue that Western Europe would never have got this far without the utopian goal or telos of "unity." Only by resolutely embracing the objective of "ever-closer union" have we reached this more modest degree of permanent institutional cooperation, with important elements of legal and economic integration. Yet as a paradigm for European policy in our time, the notion of "unification" is fundamentally flawed. The most recent period of European history provides no indication that the immensely diverse peoples of Europe-speaking such different languages, having such disparate histories, geographies, cultures, and economies-are ready to merge peacefully and voluntarily into a single polity. It provides substantial evidence of a directly countervailing trend: toward the constitution-or reconstitution-of nation-states. If unity was not attained among a small number of West European states with strong elements of common history under the paradoxically favorable conditions of the Cold War, how can we possibly expect to attain it in the infinitely larger and more diverse Europe-the whole continent-that we have to deal with after the end of the Cold War?

"Yes," a brilliant French friend said to me when I made this case to him, "I'm afraid you're right. Europe will not come to pass." "But Pierre," I replied, "you're in it!" Europe is already here, and not just as a continent. There is already a great achievement that has taken us far beyond de Gaulle's "Europe des patries" or Harold Macmillan's vision of a glorified free trade area. Yet to a degree that readers outside Europe will find hard to comprehend, European thinking about Europe is still deeply conditioned by these notions of project, process, and progress toward unification. (After all, no one talks hopefully of Africa or Asia "becoming itself.") Many Europeans are convinced that if we do not go forward toward unification, we must necessarily go backward. This view is expressed in the so-called "bicycle theory" of European integration: if you stop pedaling, the bicycle will fall over. Actually, as anyone who rides a bicycle knows, all you have to do is to put one foot back on the ground. And anyway, Europe is not a bicycle.

If we Europeans convince ourselves that not advancing further along the path to unity is tantamount to failure, we risk snatching failure from the jaws of success. For what has been achieved already in a large part of Europe is a very great success, without precedent on the European continent or contemporary equivalent on any other continent. It is as if someone had built a fine if rather rambling palace and then convinced himself that he was an abject failure because it was not the Parthenon. Yet the case is more serious and urgent than this. For today it is precisely the forced march to unity-across the "bridge too far" of monetary union-that is threatening the very achievement it is supposed to complete.

But what is the alternative? How else should we "think Europe" if not in terms of this paradigm of unification that has dominated European thinking about Europe for half a century? How can we characterize positively what we have already built in a large part of Europe, and what it is both desirable and realistic to work toward in a wider Europe? I believe the best paradigm is that of liberal order. Historically, liberal order is an attempt to avoid both the extremes between which Europe has unhappily oscillated through most of its modern history: violent disorder, on the one hand, and hegemonic order on the other-hegemonic order that itself was always built on the use of force and the denial of national and democratic aspirations within the constitutive empires or spheres of influence. Philosophically, such an order draws on the late Sir Isaiah Berlin's central liberal insight that people pursue different ends that cannot be reconciled but may peacefully coexist. It also draws on Judith Shklar's "liberalism of fear," with its deeply pessimistic view of the propensity of human beings to indulge in violence and cruelty, and on a sense that what Shklar modestly called "damage control" is the first necessity of political life. Institutionally, the EU, NATO, the

Council of Europe, and the Organization for Security and Cooperation in Europe are all building blocks of such a liberal order.

Liberal order differs from previous European orders in several vital ways. Its first commandment is the renunciation of force in the resolution of disputes between its members. Of course, this goal is an ancient one. We find it anticipated already in King George of Podebrady's great proposal of 1464 for "the inauguration of peace throughout Christendom." There we read that he and his fellow princes "shall not take up arms for the sake of any disagreements, complaints or disputes, nor shall we allow any to take up arms in our name." But today we have well-tried institutions of bourgeois internationalism in which to practice what Churchill called making "jaw-jaw" rather than "war-war."

Liberal order is, by design, non-hegemonic. To be sure, the system depends to some extent on the external hegemonic balancer, the United States-"Europe's pacifier," as more than one author has quipped. And of course, Luxembourg does not carry the same weight as Germany. But the new model order that we have developed in the EU does permit smaller states to have an influence often disproportionate to their size. A key element of this model order is the way it allows different alliances of European states on individual issues rather than cementing any fixed alliances. Another is the framework of common European law. If the European Convention on Human Rights were incorporated into the treaties of the union, as Ralf Dahrendorf has suggested, the EU would gain a much-needed element of direct responsibility for the liberties of the individual citizen.

Liberal order also differs from previous European orders in explicitly legitimating the interest of participating states in each other's internal affairs. Building on the so-called Helsinki process, it considers human, civil, and not least minority rights to be a primary and legitimate subject of international concern. These rights are to be sustained by international norms, support, and, where necessary, also pressure. Such a liberal order recognizes that there is a logic that leads peoples who speak the same language and share the same culture and tradition to want to govern themselves in their own state. There is such a thing as liberal nationalism. But it also recognizes that in many places a peaceful, neat separation into nation-states will be impossible. In such cases it acknowledges a responsibility to help sustain what may variously be called multiethnic, multicultural, or multinational democracies within an international framework. This is what we disastrously failed to do for Bosnia but can still do for Macedonia or Estonia.

Missing from this paradigm is one idea that remains very important in contemporary European visions, especially those of former great powers such as France, Britain, and Germany. This is the notion of "Europe" as a single actor on the world stage, a world power able to stand up to the United States, Russia, or China. In truth, a drive for world power is hardly more attractive because it is a joint enterprise than it was when attempted-somewhat more crudely-by individual European nations. Certainly, in a world of large trading blocs we must be able to protect our own interests. Certainly, a degree of power-projection, including the coordinated use of military power, will be needed to realize the objectives of liberal order even within the continent of Europe and in adjacent areas of vital interest to us, such as North Africa and the Middle East. But beyond this, just to put our own all-European house in order would be a large enough contribution to the well-being of the world.

Some may object that I have paid too much attention to mere semantics. Why not let the community be called a union and the process "unification," even if they are not that in reality? Vaclav Havel comes close to this position when he writes, "Today, Europe is attempting to give itself a historically new kind of order in a process that we refer to as unification." And of course I do not expect the European Union to be, so to speak, dis-named. After all, the much looser world organization of states is still called the United Nations. But the issue is far from merely semantic.

To consolidate Europe's liberal order and to spread it across the whole continent is both a more urgent and, in the light of history, a more realistic goal for Europe at the beginning of the twenty-first century than the vain pursuit of unification in a part of it. Nor, finally, is liberal order a less idealistic goal than unity. For unity is not a primary value in itself. It is but a means to higher ends. Liberal order, by contrast, directly implies not one but two primary values: peace and freedom.

Timothy Garton Ash is a Fellow of St. Antony's College, Oxford. His books include The Magic Lantern, In Europe's Name, and most recently The File: A Personal History. This essay is dedicated to the memory of Sir Isaiah Berlin.

The Importance of Being English: Eyeing the Sceptered Isles

DAVID FROMKIN

A member of the right wing National Front Party unfolds the Union Jack prior to a march to the Cenotaph during the Remembrance Day ceremonies on November 14, 1993.

On December 22, 1941, only a fortnight after the Japanese attack on Pearl Harbor brought America into World War II, British Prime Minister Winston Churchill and his entourage flew to a three-week conference in the New World codenamed Arcadia. In the course of Arcadia, the two countries agreed to establish a combined Joint Chiefs of Staff to direct their armed forces worldwide, and the British agreed that these supreme commanders should be located not in London, but in Washington. It was a partnership weighted toward the Americans: day-to-day military decisions for both countries were to be made in the United States.

In September 1943, Churchill proposed to President Franklin D. Roosevelt that after victory had been achieved, the wartime arrangement -- a joint high command located in the United States -- should continue, initially on a ten-year renewable basis, but in the hope that one day it might become permanent. "Roosevelt liked the idea at first sight," the prime minister reported to his colleagues and to King George VI.

Although Churchill often was derided as a romantic reactionary, addicted to empire and unwilling to recognize the harsh realities of the twentieth century, he showed himself on this point able and willing to face facts. He saw that the United Kingdom was losing its place as the world's foremost power -- permanently. Relative economic decline was the main cause; it also was part of the price that fate exacted from Britain for having fought the German wars from start to finish. Changes in the ranks of great powers are normal in history. What is unusual -- perhaps even unique -- is that Britain relinquished its top position to its successor consciously and, to the extent that it had a choice, voluntarily.

At the time, not all British officials agreed that global supremacy had been lost. In 1945 it was the view of the Foreign Office that Britain "possesses all the skill and resources required to recover a dominating place in the economic world." But Sir Henry Tizard, chief scientific adviser to the Ministry of Defense, came closer to the mark a few years later when he wrote, "We persist in regarding ourselves as a great power, capable of everything and only temporarily handicapped by economic difficulties. [But] we are not a great power and never will be again."

Churchill had evidently hoped to maintain his country's global dominance by leaning on the Americans. But his Labour successors in office (1945-51) chose instead to wind down Britain's commitments when they found they could no longer afford them.

ONE FINE DAY

Surprisingly, the exact date and place at which Britain handed over leadership to the United States has been pinpointed both by participants and by historians. It was in Washington in the late afternoon of Friday, February 21, 1947 -- a cold, gray, and rainy day -- that the first secretary of the British embassy delivered to the Department of State a note that later was to become famous. The note told then Secretary of State General George C. Marshall that Great Britain no longer could shore up the free world's positions in the eastern Mediterranean in the face of a threatening Soviet Union. British aid to Greece and Turkey would terminate on March 31. If the United States wished to take Britain's place, it should prepare to do so effective April 1.

In a burst of energy and creativity, the American government took hold of the torch and ran with it, formulating the Truman Doctrine, the Greek-Turkish aid program, and the Marshall Plan. Europe reacted positively, for which a major part of the credit must go to Britain's Ernest Bevin, foreign secretary in Clement Attlee's Labour administration. Like many Western European and American leaders at the time, he feared that the United States would withdraw into isolation after the Second

World War, as it had after the First. It was Bevin who initiated the European response to the Marshall Plan. It was Bevin, too, who organized a European mutual defense league; and after Norway asked for support when threatened by the Soviets in 1948, it was Bevin who drew in the Americans to form NATO. For a few episodes in 1947-48, Britain played the role in world affairs that the United States wanted it to play, and America played the part that Britain wanted for it.

But from there on, their paths diverged. The role of the United States grew over the years. Before long America had a presence in most parts of the world. Instead of believing, as they once had, that nothing outside the western hemisphere concerned them, Americans came to believe that almost everything everywhere was their business. They entered a global conflict with the Soviet Union, one superpower against another, and ultimately emerged as the leader not just of the West, but of the world.

LORD OF THE RINGS

Less well explored, until now, is the story of how Britain missed its chance to adopt a new role in world politics as Europe's leader. The distinguished British journalist Hugo Young has provided a definitive account of how successive prime ministers, other politicians, and civil servants failed to meet that challenge. It should become the authoritative narrative, the point of reference in its field.

As Young tells it, Churchill left Britons a dazzling vision -- but one that became an excuse for strategic indecision. In Churchill's view, Britain was to be at the center of three concentric circles: a Europe that would unite, a commonwealth and empire that would cohere, and a United States that would serve as Britain's partner.

Yet by the war's end, one of the options was on the verge of becoming untenable. The Attlee government embarked on a program of dissolving the empire. India received independence. Later the Tory government of Macmillan and Macleod pushed forward decolonization in Africa as well.

Politically the empire ceased to exist as a cohesive unit. And in a world that aimed at free trade, the tariff barriers that bound the Commonwealth economically threatened to become an anachronism. So whereas in the first half of the twentieth century, Great Britain still played a central role on the world stage as leader of a commonwealth and an empire, in the latter half both had disintegrated and the role had become ceremonial.

EUROPEAN (DIS)UNION

The second of Churchill's concentric circles was to be the community of Europe. It leaped into existence in May 1950, when French Foreign Minister Robert Schuman proposed the creation of the European Coal and Steel Community, a plan conceived of by France's postwar economic comissioner, Jean Monnet, welcomed by German Chancellor Konrad Adenauer, and supported by U.S. Secretary of State Dean

Acheson. The plan for combining basic industries was the first step toward merging continental Europe's economies with the aim, among others, of preventing future wars.

Ernest Bevin balked. The Schuman Plan had been sprung on him as a surprise. It looked like a plot, a continental cartel, and aroused all sorts of English prejudices in him. By joining Europe, Britain might have taken the lead, but it chose instead to watch, to wait -- and to obstruct.

The European movement went forward anyway. It thrived. Time and again, Britain had a chance both to join it and to lead. There was a strong economic argument for becoming European. But the British remained reluctant to throw in their lot unreservedly with their neighbors, fearing for their independence and special character. When the United Kingdom finally moved to enter Europe, French President Charles de Gaulle barred the way. In the end, the United Kingdom got in in 1973, but as a dissenter, inclined to oppose moves toward further unification.

For hundreds of years, Britain has opposed the unification of the continent under one dominant power, seeing in it a threat to the vital interests of an island nation. England fought Louis XIV and Napoleon, whose Continental System excluded the British isles from European trade. Young quotes de Gaulle's memoirs on a meeting with Harold Macmillan: "The Common Market is the Continental System all over again," the British prime minister told his old friend, the French president. "Britain cannot accept it," Macmillan told him. "I beg you to give it up."

Young has interviewed extensively and tells a tale of Foreign Office officials and other civil servants as well as prime ministers and cabinet members. He offers a full and complete account, a sad tale of official waffling, missed chances, and human frailties. Faced with one of the greatest questions in their country's history, the few British officials who were wise and brave emerge with all the greater credit.

A QUESTION OF CHARACTER

Reluctant to become European, many in British public life advocated an alternative alliance: the special relationship with the United States. A second argument against joining Europe often voiced was that it might jeopardize that relationship.

But it was not there to jeopardize. Repeatedly, America's leaders made it clear that this option was not available. The most frequently repeated statement of the American position was given by Dean Acheson when addressing a student conference at West Point in 1962: "Great Britain has lost an empire and has not yet found a role. The attempt to play a separate power role, that is, a role apart from Europe, a role based primarily on a 'special relationship' with the United States, a role based on being head of the Commonwealth," is "about played out." The former secretary of state spoke at the time only as a private citizen. Yet his words carried weight, and accurately stated the American view.

The reality of national character is sometimes questioned, yet it is difficult to discount. Its existence, as Hans Morgenthau wrote long ago in Politics Among Nations, is "contested but ... incontestable." Any discussion of Britain's relationship with the continent of Europe -- the only area in which Acheson allowed the British a role to play -- tends to end in an appreciation of how different Britons are from everybody else.

Ian Buruma considers Britain's relationship with Europe in that cultural context. In Anglomania he explores the notion of what it is to be British according to foreigners. It is a rewarding undertaking; Britain has had, and continues to have, such an odd character in the eyes of others. The non-British are fascinated by British whimsy, baÛed by British humor and eccentricity, and filled with admiration for British good-sportsmanship.

In her centuries as a top player in international politics, Britannia has made her share of enemies. What is striking is how many admirable traits foreigners nonetheless project on the English, and how widespread has been the passion for Englishness. All over the world, among peoples of various nationality, race, language, and religion, there are those who, regarding themselves as exceptional, believe that, deep down, they are English gentlemen.

Buruma recounts that Theodor Herzl, the father of Zionism, in sketching out the utopia he planned to establish, provided that "all boys born in the Jewish state would learn to play cricket." In a similar spirit, Pierre de Coubertin (1863-1937), founder of the modern Olympic games, decided to instill the spirit of fair play in his countrymen by introducing cricket into France.

But can Englishness be taught? Beneath the wonderful charm and gentle humor of Buruma's very personal book, filled with family anecdotes, lies that serious question. Buruma, who makes reading a pleasure and writing seem easy, entertains but also aims to instruct. He wants Britain to join Europe. He believes that Europe can change Britain for the better. But he also believes Britain can change Europe for the better: he wants the British to bring their special virtues of moderation, good sense, and humor into the great mix. But for that to work, Englishness must be exportable.

Buruma shows that whether Englishness is in fact exportable is the question on which all else depends, in assessing Britain's role in Europe's future -- and vice versa. But Anglomania is too tentative, too slight, too unsystematic -- dare one say, too English? -- to provide a definite answer, let alone a definitive one.

Just as much of the world has glorified Great Britain, there is also a book to be written about how the British, over the course of history, have defined themselves. Here, too, there would be much whimsy and eccentricity. More seriously, there would be traits that led to distinctive traditions in law and politics: traits that usually have been defined in terms of differences from continental Europeans.

The English Channel is not very wide. Even in earlier times, it did not provide much of a barrier. Julius Caesar crossed it, as did the legions of the emperor Claudius, who brought the Roman occupation. Centuries later, Angles, Saxons, and other Germanic tribes found their way to Britain's shores and swept over the land when the Romans left. Vikings raided in their longboats more than a millennium ago. William the Conqueror crossed from Normandy in 1066, bringing the British isles into the ambit of French and therefore continental politics.

In the Elizabethan era or thereabouts the English separated themselves from the continent by developing sea power. From then on, the islanders defended themselves by controlling the Channel rather than their own shoreline: the sinking of the Spanish Armada in 1588 (even if an act of fate) was the symbolic beginning of that. The oceans provided the country, as a nascent sea power, with almost endless frontiers. And in repelling the Hapsburg empire, England stood for freedom, for the independence of smaller countries, and against all that was associated with the Spanish Inquisition. These strands were woven into the national myth.

In the seventeenth century the English took on new characteristics. After much political experimentation, they settled on moderate, liberal, constitutional democracy -- and came to believe, with John Locke, that an ancient and not entirely relevant Magna Carta guaranteed them the rule of law. The law in which they believed, moreover, was not the code of a divine or imperial lawgiver, but the Common Law: ancient wisdom, precedent, accreted case by case, the product of experience rather than pure logic.

This was how the British saw their character in law, government, and politics. It stood in stark contrast to that of France and the continent, their supposed partners in European union. France, for example, saw itself as Cartesian, ruthlessly logical; it governed from the center and micromanaged, passing laws based on principle rather than experience. And it was the British, not the European, approach that was handed down to and shared with the United States of America.

OVER HERE

Acheson said that Britain never really had a choice between entering Europe and maintaining the special relationship with America. Hugo Young clearly believes that too, and quotes with approval Britain's current prime minister, Tony Blair, who said (in 1995) that Britain's role was to be "a major global player," but that it could fulfill that role only by using Europe as a base. Blair, Young tells us, was the first prime minister "elected on a ticket that said he was entirely comfortable to be a European." His coming to power was, in Young's view, the end of a half century of refusing to face reality. True enough, and yet Blair has not turned away from America in order to do so. He enjoys at least as special a relationship with the United States as did Margaret Thatcher and is looked on by the White House as a partner.

Adversaries in the eighteenth and nineteenth centuries, Britain and America became allies early in the twentieth. They had always shared beliefs and values, language and literature; but theirs was less than a full alliance while their respective power standings remained in flux and while they engaged in cutthroat trade rivalry. That came to an end during and after the Second World War.

Yet even after the war, the United States still had one major quarrel with its mother country, one important enough to prevent a full alliance: the existence of the British Empire. America was always opposed to Europe's possession of overseas colonial empires, and showed it unmistakably over Suez in 1956, when the United States stood with the Soviet Union against Britain and France. Britain's dissolution of its empire in the 1960s changed the transatlantic dynamics. Now, in policies as in beliefs, the United Kingdom and the United States could be in full accord. Partnership finally became possible and remains so today.

CONVOCATION OF THE GYRES

The creation of a European union seemed a wildly improbable project in 1945. Yet here it is in 1999. Britain would be wise to play a full role in it, and to try to mitigate some of the EU's less attractive features (such as overcentralization and excessive bureaucracy).

But no longer is the American option, another of Churchill's concentric circles, unavailable. In fact, the partnership between the two countries has been revived. The Atlantic alliance is not merely available today; it is flourishing, as the world saw in the Kosovo campaign -- whatever its other merits or lack thereof.

Nor need a choice between allies be made; again, Churchill seems to have been right. The two spheres are not mutually exclusive. Ian Buruma suggests that Britain should commit to Europe in part because it has so much of value to contribute to the EU. But Britain as a partner may also have a great deal to contribute to the United States, including wisdom, restraint, humor, and experience. Is there really any reason for Britain to choose between Europe and America? Isn't there enough Englishness to go around?

David Fromkin is Professor of International Relations, History, and Law at Boston University and author, most recently, of Kosovo Crossing: American Ideals Meet Reality on the Balkan Battlefields.

What If the British Vote No?

Charles Grant

A bus painted with Anti-EU Constitution message passes Westminster Abbey as guests arrive for a royal service in London on June 2, 2003.

EU CONSTITUTION AT STAKE

In June 2004, the member states of the European Union concluded the negotiation of a treaty that, if ratified, would establish a European constitution that would make substantive changes to the way the union works. For the first time, an individual would be appointed president of the European Council, overseeing the regular summits of the heads of government of the EU nations and their foreign ministers. The EU would itself have a foreign minister. The amended rules on majority voting would allow a measure to pass if 55 percent of the member states were in favor, so long as they represented 65 percent of the EU's population. And the EU would gain new powers in justice and home affairs, requiring cooperation among interior ministries on immigration, asylum, crime, and justice.

The governments of all 25 countries have signed the treaty, but it cannot take effect unless ratified by each member state, through parliamentary vote or referendum. Ten EU countries have chosen to hold referendums. In February, the Spanish voted 77 percent in favor. A similar margin of victory is expected in Portugal and Luxembourg. Approval is less certain in the forthcoming French, Dutch, Polish, Danish, Irish, and Czech referendums, although opinion polls point to a positive result in all those countries. Only in the United Kingdom do the polls suggest that a majority will vote no. But that vote alone would throw the EU into a constitutional crisis.

Any initiative to salvage the constitutional treaty at that point would face huge political and legal obstacles. Some member states would probably try to push ahead and exclude the United Kingdom from the EU. Alternatively, France and Germany might seek to establish a "hard core" of states committed to a closer union, a new organization that would coexist within the broader EU. More plausibly, however, sets of ambitious countries might set up several different vanguard groups to facilitate closer cooperation in particular policy areas. Thus, Europe would have not a hard core but a "messy core": it would not be tightly organized, and the various groups would not all consist of the same members. In the long run, the countries that took part in all these groups would emerge as the EU's leadership.

Such a development would not bode well for either the EU's future or transatlantic relations. If a messy core emerged within the EU, the United Kingdom and other U.S. allies, such as Poland, would likely wind up outside of it. Europe would spend several years trying to sort out its institutions, rather than cope with the many security, economic, and environmental challenges that it faces. The EU would stop enlarging. And its chances of pressing ahead with economic reform or developing a coherent foreign policy would diminish dramatically.

LIVING ON THE EDGE

People from other countries are often puzzled by the fervor of the United Kingdom's hostility to the EU, or its "Euroskepticism." Ever since the British joined what is now called the European Union, in 1973, their relationship with that club has been troubled. For almost the entire period, one of the country's two main political parties has supported either loosening ties to the union or breaking them altogether. Although the Conservative Party took the United Kingdom into the union, its internal arguments over European policy destroyed the government of Margaret Thatcher, weakened that of John Major, and contributed to the party's general election defeats in 1997 and 2001. The Conservative Party now wants to "renegotiate" the terms of the United Kingdom's membership, while some of its leaders advocate outright withdrawal. Meanwhile, the current, pro-European position of the Labour Party, which abandoned its policy of quitting the EU in the mid-1980s, is unpopular. Labour will probably win the general election expected in May 2005 but lose the constitutional referendum planned for mid-2006. Such a defeat would destroy its credibility as a governing party.

Opinion polls show that, if given the choice, around four out of ten Britons would vote to leave the EU and that an overwhelming majority oppose the constitutional treaty. Such attitudes are deeply rooted in U.K. history, geography, and economics. Being an island on the edge of Europe, the United Kingdom has for the past 400 years developed close ties to other continents. Winston Churchill once said to Charles de Gaulle, "When I have to choose between you and Roosevelt, you should know that I will always choose Roosevelt. And when I have to choose between Europe and the wide open seas, you should know that I will always choose the wide open seas." World War II still shapes the way many Britons view their country and its relationship with the continent. The British had a more glorious war than most other Europeans, and their newspapers and television programs seldom let them forget it.

Recent economic success has also reinforced a sense of self-sufficiency among the British. For the past dozen years, the U.K. economy has outperformed those of France, Germany, and Italy. The United Kingdom's economic growth rate has been about one percentage point higher than those of France, Germany, and Italy, while its unemployment rate is half theirs. Unlike those three countries, the United Kingdom opted out of the euro, the European currency launched in 1999, and apparently has prospered by keeping the pound.

Leaving aside long-term trends, there are immediate reasons why Britons opposed to the constitutional treaty are confident of a referendum victory. The press is on their side. Three out of every four newspapers sold in the United Kingdom are extremely hostile to the EU and its constitution. Much of their reporting of the constitution's drawbacks is exaggerated, and some of it is false. Popular newspapers claim, for example, that the constitution would force the United Kingdom to give up its seat on the United Nations Security Council; that Brussels bureaucrats would command British troops, control British oil reserves, and regulate British borders; and that the EU would gain new powers to interfere in the U.K. labor market. None of these points is true, but the popular press knows how to frighten people. Of course, some of the horror stories are real: the EU's administration has been tarnished by corruption scandals, and the Common Agricultural Policy, although reformed, continues to swallow more than 40 percent of the EU budget. But instead of reporting these flaws in a measured and evenhanded tone, popular papers tend to portray the EU as a conspiracy led by France and Germany to promote their interests against those of the United Kingdom.

Furthermore, advertisements in the media routinely attack the EU constitution, while none support it. The various anti-EU lobbying groups are well organized and well funded. Their combined budgets are probably between five and ten times greater than the $1.25 million spent in 2004 by the United Kingdom's single pro-EU lobbying group, called Britain in Europe. Traditionally, British business leaders have been pro-European, and particularly pro-euro. But they have been angered by the Labour government's failure to deliver on its promise to hold a referendum on the currency, and they refuse to fund the pro-constitution campaign unless the government leads the way. So far, however, Downing Street has kept quiet: its priority is to win the general election expected in May. Only then will the government try to convince people to support the constitution.

Does the new treaty have any chance of passing? Possibly. Pro-Europeans have not given up hope of winning the referendum. They expect that when the government does finally start trying to win support for the constitution, money will flow into their organizations. They believe they will be able to reveal many of the Euroskeptics' claims to be false and that many voters will ultimately look less to the popular press for information on the treaty than to the BBC, which will be more objective. And if the rest of the EU has endorsed the treaty by the time the United Kingdom votes, the British people may start to fear isolation. If Britons believe that a vote for the constitution is a vote for the status quo -- and that a vote against would create chaos and uncertainty -- they could conceivably endorse the treaty. But the odds remain slim. Most political commentators continue to predict that British voters will reject the new constitution.

THE DAY AFTER TOMORROW

If the British do decide to vote no, but the other member states adopt the treaty, the future of the EU could take one of six courses. The first possibility is that nothing would happen. The other countries would accept the death of the constitutional treaty and would simply continue operating with the existing treaties. This outcome, however, is not plausible: most EU governments do not like the existing treaties and believe that the newly enlarged union -- ten countries joined in May 2004 -- will not run smoothly without the constitution.

Second, the member states could choose to renegotiate the constitutional treaty. A new intergovernmental conference could cut out the most controversial parts, making it more palatable to British tastes. But this option is no more realistic than the first. Many governments fear that revisiting the hard-fought compromises enshrined in the treaty could result in a less attractive deal. Having already made big concessions to the United Kingdom to ensure that Prime Minister Tony Blair would sign, they are not prepared to give away any more. Nor would they want to go through the ratification process all over again.

Under a third scenario, the British would hold a second referendum on the constitutional treaty, as the Danes did after first rejecting the Maastricht Treaty in 1992 and as the Irish did after voting against the Nice Treaty in 2001. In this case, however, such a stratagem would not make sense. Because the Maastricht Treaty extended the EU's role in defense, immigration, and monetary policy, the Danes could be offered ways out of those three areas before a second vote. Similarly, the EU was able to guarantee Ireland's neutral status, to appease those Irish who worried that the Nice Treaty's provisions on defense would compromise their neutrality. The trouble with the constitutional treaty is that it mainly covers matters impossible for a single member to bypass: EU institutions and voting rules. In the one area in which it does extend significant EU powers -- justice and home affairs -- the United Kingdom is already free not to adopt union measures.

Three more-likely scenarios remain. One would be for the other 24 member states to enact the treaty, forcing the British to leave the EU. Some prominent continental politicians, such as former French President Valéry Giscard d'Estaing and former French Finance Minister Nicolas Sarkozy, say that the British should not be allowed to block the treaty. Legally, the 24 cannot adopt the treaty without British ratification, but there may be a way around that obstacle. The 24 could withdraw from the existing

EU treaties, redraft the constitutional treaty among themselves, and then sign and ratify it. (The 1969 Vienna Convention on international treaties allows signatories to withdraw in certain circumstances, although there is some legal doubt as to how this process would work.) The United Kingdom would then have to negotiate an associate status similar to that of Norway and Switzerland, which enjoy access to the EU market but cannot vote on its rules.

The British may assume that they are too special to be cast adrift. They should not. For the EU's more integrationist countries, the United Kingdom has been a constant bother, often thwarting schemes for a more united Europe. If the Conservative Party and the popular press used their referendum victory as a springboard to campaign for quitting the EU; if British politicians of all parties sought popularity through cheap attacks on Paris, Berlin, and Brussels; and if the government lacked the mettle to oppose them, the United Kingdom would find itself friendless.

Yet any effort to exclude the British would only succeed if all 24 states backed it, and the United Kingdom's xenophobic ranting would have to be quite extreme to drive them all away. And if, in the wake of a negative referendum, London made an effort to consult with Europe on how to deal with the crisis, it would keep its friends. Many EU members want to build a stronger common foreign and security policy and to improve the union's record on economic reform, and they know that both tasks would be harder without London. Countries that share the United Kingdom's Atlanticism and market-oriented approach to economics would also think twice before ostracizing the British. Countries such as Portugal, the Netherlands, Poland, and the Nordic and Baltic states would not relish the prospects of an EU dominated by France and Germany. It is thus relatively unlikely that the United Kingdom would be pushed out of the union.

Under the fifth scenario, France, Germany, and their allies would accept that the constitutional treaty cannot be implemented without British ratification. Instead, they would set up a new organization, with its own institutions, for the EU states that want a real political union. This "hard core" of countries would harmonize their policies in areas such as taxes, legal procedures, and research and development. And they would try to establish a European criminal court and merge their armed forces and diplomatic services. This group would have its own budget, secretariat, council of ministers, and parliamentary assembly. It would coexist with the broader EU.

But it would be immensely difficult, legally and politically, not only to establish such a core but also to ensure that it operated smoothly alongside the EU. If the United Kingdom does vote no on the constitution, there would be strong support in France for a core Europe. Prominent French politicians, such as President Jacques Chirac and leading socialists Laurent Fabius and Dominique Strauss-Kahn, have already voiced their support. But the scheme would not be viable without equally strong German support. Although Chancellor Gerhard Schröder is thought to be sympathetic to the idea of a European hard core, many Germans remain less than enthusiastic. Foreign Minister Joschka Fischer announced a similar plan in 2000 and subsequently withdrew it, arguing that only a broad EU of continental scale could cope with current strategic challenges. The Christian Democratic opposition is divided. The German finance and defense ministries are opposed. So is most of the German business community, which fears that forging a closer relationship with France at the expense of the United Kingdom, the United States, and others could hurt the German economy.

Moreover, the core would be hugely divisive, upsetting those countries left on the outside. EU institutions would probably be hostile to the core group, seeing it as a rival center of authority. In some circumstances, the activities of the core could even breach European law. If core members favored one another in business matters, for example, other EU states could seek redress from the European Court of Justice.

The fact that Paris and Berlin would lead the core would in itself create problems. The pair revived their close alliance in 2002, after five years of frequently being at odds. Since then, they have often sparked resentment from other EU members, for example by breaking the rules on budget deficits in the Stability and Growth Pact and agreeing to preserve existing levels of spending in the Common Agricultural Policy. Some EU governments believe that France and Germany's cooperation serves to promote their own narrow interests rather than the wider European good.

In the end, a sixth scenario is the one most likely to unfold if the constitution fails the British referendum: the emergence of a "messy core." If attempts to exclude the United Kingdom or to establish a hard core come to nothing, the integrationist countries will seek to promote a more united Europe in a number of ways, including by trying to implement parts of the constitutional treaty. Although most parts, such as the new voting rules, cannot be implemented without ratification, some, such as the provision for the establishment of a European diplomatic service, can be applied without breaching the current treaties. The integrationist countries could also try to salvage other novel elements of the constitution by holding a mini-intergovernmental conference and trying to amend the existing treaties, adopting, for example, the new rules on majority voting. Such a scheme would, however, require every member state to sign and ratify the treaty amendments. The British government, in the wake of a referendum defeat, might find that difficult.

What the United Kingdom could not do is stop the integrationist countries from using current EU rules to establish vanguard groups in particular policy areas, for example, in corporate taxation or research and development. Nor could London prevent the creation of other vanguard groups outside the EU framework, in areas such as border guards, police cooperation, and criminal justice. There is a precedent: the "Schengen area" of passport-free travel was established by France, Germany, and the three Benelux countries in the 1980s as an entity separate from the EU, although in 1997 the union took it over. The integrationists would also likely build the euro group, currently an informal forum for the countries in the single currency, into a solid institution.

The consequence of all this would be further European integration, some of it involving the whole EU, but much of it within distinct but overlapping smaller groups. Eventually, the countries that belonged to all the groups would start to caucus, attempt to guide and direct the whole union, and probably establish their own secretariat. Europe would thus develop a messy core. Messy or not, however, the long-term effects would be similar to those of a hard core: the EU would be divided into two groups of countries, with France and Germany dominating the center group and the United Kingdom relegated to the outer circle.

THE BUTTERFLY EFFECT

Ever since it joined the union, the United Kingdom has been an influential member, well placed to represent U.S. interests, when it so chooses. But stuck in an outer circle of the EU, the British would be less able to nudge union policies in an Atlanticist direction. (The same applies to other close U.S. allies, such as Poland and the Baltic countries, which are unlikely to join the core.) The United Kingdom would lose influence not only over the policy areas covered by the core, but also over those that remained under the EU's general ambit. Indeed, bound together by common interests, the core countries would likely support each other even in fields that involved all the EU members. Such mutual back-scratching has been evident in the past between France and Germany: at the Berlin EU summit in March 1999, because of Germany's broader interest in maintaining its alliance with France, Schröder let Chirac unravel a radical reform of the Common Agricultural Policy that Germany (and the United Kingdom) supported.

British rejection of the constitution would also halt further EU enlargement. The United States has always, with good reason, favored expanding the EU, understanding that the process helps spread security, democracy, and prosperity. But the union can only negotiate the entry of new members when it has clearly defined rules and stable institutions. French politicians have stated explicitly that the EU cannot admit new nations unless the constitutional treaty is implemented. They have a point: the basic purpose of the treaty is to reform EU institutions so that they can accommodate more members. Bulgaria and Romania, due to join in 2007, are so close to membership that they will probably get in no matter what happens with the constitution. But the treaty's rejection would scuttle talks with Turkey and Croatia, which are due to start this year, and force Ukraine and countries in the western Balkans to postpone their membership ambitions. It is true that in the long run, if the constitution were abandoned and a core established, the EU member states would probably not object to further enlargement -- but only so long as the aspirants did not join the core.

Economically, a European core dominated by Paris and Berlin would likely lean toward defensive or possibly protectionist economic policies that would not be in Washington's best interests. Most of the union's more dynamic economies -- those of the United Kingdom, Poland, and the Nordic and Baltic countries -- would be outside the central group. There are, of course, successful companies and industries in France and Germany, but both countries have been plagued by slow growth and high unemployment, and they have lagged behind in the EU's "Lisbon process" of economic reform (the member states have committed to reaching a series of economic targets and are supposed to achieve them through peer-group pressure, among other means). Although the core would probably not inflict great damage on the broader European market, the overall credibility of the Lisbon process would suffer if the leadership group consisted mainly of foot-draggers. The core countries' efforts to maintain high levels of worker protection and company taxation could harm their competitiveness with eastern Europe's low-tax, lightly regulated economies. Europe's leaders would be unlikely to push the continent to abandon the policies that have led to low growth and high unemployment.

A core led by France and Germany would also have its own approach to foreign policy, which would be relatively anti-American (although that could change after the German general election in the fall of 2006 and the French presidential election the following summer). The countries that were most hostile to the Iraq war -- France, Germany, Belgium, Luxembourg, and, following the electoral victory of President José Luis Rodriguez Zapatero, Spain -- would be in the forefront of any core. Led by Chirac and Schröder, the core countries would promote a multipolar world, with Europe as one emerging pole. At the same time, the EU's periphery, including the United Kingdom and Poland, would tend toward Atlanticism. With that kind of split foreign policy, Europe could not develop into a more effective strategic actor. To be sure, some in the Bush administration would be quite happy to see Europe remain divided, so that they could play the various member states off of one another. But others -- including Secretary of State Condoleezza Rice, to judge from her comments in Europe in February -- stress that Washington needs Europe to help it tackle global security threats. They understand that a divided Europe cannot be a useful strategic partner.

The British have long played a pivotal role in helping the Americans and continental Europeans understand each other. If the United Kingdom becomes alienated from the continent and its leadership core, transatlantic relations will suffer. Washington is more likely to listen to, and respect, a Europe that is strong and whole. The Bush administration should pay serious attention to the ratification of the EU's constitutional treaty. When appropriate, the White House should even urge the peoples of Europe to adopt it. The treaty's implementation would not radically change the way the EU works. But if the treaty were rejected by a large member state such as the United Kingdom, the ensuing crisis would turn the union inwards, toward endless institutional negotiations, and away from the global challenges that the United States and Europe need to face together. Such a weak and divided Europe would strengthen the hand of unilateralists in the United States and of Europeans eager to work against Washington's interests.

Charles Grant is Director of the Centre for European Reform in London and the author of What Happens If Britain Votes No? Ten Ways Out of a European Constitutional Crisis.

The End of Europe?

Laurent Cohen-Tanugi

Workers erect scaffolding at the famous Fori Imperiali in Rome October 25, 2004, just days before the Heads of State and Government and Foreign Ministers of 29 European countries met at the Campidoglio to sign the Treaty and Final Act that established a Constitution for Europe. The treaty was adandoned the next year.

THE GREAT DEPRESSION

After French and Dutch voters rejected the draft treaty establishing a constitution for Europe last spring, there was no doubt that a crisis of unprecedented seriousness confronted the European Union. The shock was so severe that the ratification process was extended for an indefinite "period of reflection," to allow some EU members (such as the United Kingdom) to suspend further votes that might deal the treaty additional blows. Soon, however, the effects of the French and Dutch no votes were compounded by the European Council's failure to agree on the EU budget for 2007-

13 thanks to a Franco-British showdown over the financial rebate to the United Kingdom and the Common Agricultural Policy. This double fiasco triggered concern that even the past achievements of European economic integration once held to be irreversible, such as the single market and the euro, might come undone. Europe has been in a state of depression in the months since.

There are good reasons to be alarmed, but one should not misdiagnose the problem and mistake the symptoms of the EU's crisis for its causes. Disagreement over the constitution did not precipitate the EU's current troubles; rather, it was a growing malaise over the EU's operation and prospects that precipitated the constitutional debacle. The constitution's rejection by founding members of the EU does not in itself spell the end of the union, but it both reflects and deepens a profound crisis in the process of European unification -- one that has no obvious solution and carries significant implications for the United States.

A FRENCH EXCEPTION?

To outside observers, the present stalemate may appear to be just another in the long series of crises that have paved the way toward European unification. This pattern is evident in the EU's repeated deadlocks over its finances: negotiating the seven-year budget always involves tough posturing, extensive bargaining, and temporary breakdowns. The latest exercise was further complicated by increased financial burdens resulting from last year's eastward enlargement and the unwillingness of the richer member states (including some of those that pressed for enlargement) to increase or even to maintain their current contribution levels.

In other ways, too, the blow to the constitution is less severe than it might at first seem. There have been other ratification accidents in the past, such as the Danes' rejection of the Maastricht Treaty in 1992. (Danish voters ratified the treaty the following year after Denmark was allowed to opt out of some of its provisions.) True, the constitution's rejection by France and the Netherlands, two founding members of the European Community, the EU's ancestor, comes with a sharper sting. And given the contradictory reasons behind the rejection, it is difficult to imagine what adjustments or exceptions would ease the text's ratification in the future. But the no votes in France and the Netherlands had less to do with the constitution itself than with widespread frustration over economic and social ills at home, growing opposition to the ruling parties, and fears of large-scale trends such as globalization and immigration that were wrongly attributed to "Europe."

More important, hardly any of the treaty's new substance was debated during the French and Dutch referendum campaigns. The absence of a well-focused discussion only compounded the effect of the potent misrepresentation that surrounded the text from the beginning. As EU analysts will recall, the original purpose of what became the European constitution was a long overdue reform of the EU's institutions and decision-making processes, which had become increasingly unmanageable following successive waves of EU enlargement. After several attempts to streamline the union's operations failed (such as the treaties of Amsterdam [1997] and Nice [2000]), a convention of over 100 political representatives from the current 25 member states was convened. Following more than 18 months of negotiations under the chairmanship of former French President Valéry Giscard d'Estaing, delegates reached an agreement over a broad range of institutional issues and political matters.

The process took a dangerous turn early on, when the convention set out to "write a Constitution for Europe" instead of using its broad mandate to launch a Europe-wide debate over what the EU's purposes and policies should be in the twenty-first century. The lengthy document ultimately submitted for ratification in early 2005 had four parts, but only the first contained the bulk of the institutional reforms negotiated by the union's 25 members during the constitutional convention. Part II incorporated into the EU's legal framework the European Charter of Fundamental Rights adopted in 2000; Part III restated, with more coherence and certain improvements, existing EU treaty law; and Part IV contained provisions applicable only to the treaty itself, regarding amendment and ratification procedures. The convention had failed to produce a true constitution: the new treaty is indistinguishable from its predecessors from a legal standpoint. But the extensive hype surrounding the highly symbolic project set the public's expectations -- and fears -- too high. The text had been oversold to the European public before it was even presented to it.

After that, the constitution fell victim to domestic politics. A clever, ad hoc opposition -- to the treaty, European integration, EU enlargement, the market economy, globalization, and some national governments -- took advantage of the public's mixed feelings about Europe by obscuring the basic fact that the constitutional convention's rational and well-intentioned central objective had been to address some of the EU's shortcomings and distill its main tenets into a single comprehensive and streamlined document. It would be simplistic to pretend that the French (or the Dutch, for that matter) merely voted against their government when they rejected the treaty. But they certainly did not vote on, or have grounds to reject, anything the treaty would have brought about. In France at least, opponents to the text focused almost exclusively on Part III, the existing body of EU treaty law and policies, some of which dates back to the Treaty of Rome of 1957. The no campaign, orchestrated within the Socialist Party by former Prime Minister Laurent Fabius, targeted the market-economy principles that have long underlain the European community's competition policy and its single market. On the one hand, it argued that the provisions of Part III, although long standing, took on a new meaning at odds with French interests when presented in a document with an enhanced constitutional status and in the context of EU enlargement and globalization. On the other hand, the no coalition claimed that because the truly novel sections of the treaty (contained in Part I) did little to respond to Europe's needs and challenges, its definitive burial would not be the end of the EU. By simultaneously undermining Part I and demonizing Part III, no-campaigners gave voters ample reason to mistrust the treaty and no reason to fear the consequences of rejecting it. Given the French public's traditional distrust of the market and its lack of familiarity with the complexities of Europolitics, the strategy worked.

THE CRISIS BELOW

Many Europeans believe that the treaty will ultimately be ratified in one form or another; others argue that the EU will survive with or without it. They may be right, but they are missing the point. A constitutional treaty designed by a former French president and modestly advancing the goals of European integration would not have been rejected by the citizens of two committed founding members of the EU if they had been confident about the EU's condition and its ability to solve their problems. The debacle is significant evidence, therefore, that the European project is undergoing the most serious crisis of its half-century history. The French and Dutch votes did not produce the crisis; they simply brought it to the surface and then aggravated it. It was the economic, social, and political shortcomings of the existing EU that brought about the rejection of the treaty, not the other way around.

Although in some ways the no vote was more an expression of distrust of domestic politics than of disaffection with the constitution itself, the referendum debates did center on the European project and its impact on peoples' future. With Part III recapitulating 50 years of European integration, moreover, the referendum gave voters their first-ever opportunity to challenge formally and directly core features of the EU: its competition policy, the freedom-of-movement rules in the single market (notably the liberalization of services), the euro and the EU's monetary policy, and enlargement. The prereferendum debates also reflected dissatisfaction with slow growth and high unemployment, immigration, enlargement and "social dumping" from new members, the prospect of Turkish membership, globalization, and the growing competition from China and the United States. They revealed profound worry about Europe's ability to address these concerns, especially as a group of 25 heterogeneous members increasingly unable to act efficiently and with no stable geographic or cultural borders in sight. Never mind that the constitutional treaty improved the institutional framework and decision-making process of the EU and did little else. In classic French tradition, voters blamed Europe for their domestic economic ills and, by extension, the treaty for failing to remedy and perhaps reinforcing Europe's allegedly nefarious effects.

Rejecting the treaty could hardly have been the cure, of course, but the gesture itself suggests that European unification is indeed in a state of crisis -- to a degree that has not always been properly recognized within or outside of Europe. More than anything, what drove the no votes was the EU's poor economic performance and uncertain long-term prospects. Although measures of economic well-being vary significantly among European states (largely as a result of domestic rather than EU policies), the EU as a whole and the eurozone in particular have consistently suffered from a serious growth deficit vis-à-vis the United States and remain plagued with slow growth, high unemployment, and public deficits. Europe lags substantially behind the United States in investment in research and development, technological innovation, and, since 1995, productivity gains. Various demographic trends and their impact on public finances and social programs, combined with global competition, seem to condemn Europe, in the long run, to being economically marginalized by the United States, as well as China and other emerging markets.

The much-celebrated Lisbon agenda of March 2000 was intended to turn the EU into "the most competitive knowledge-based economy in the world by 2010." But halfway down the road, its ambitions are less than half met. The EU continues to fail in fulfilling such hopes largely because the structural reforms needed to improve its economic performance remain the province of national governments and require strong and coordinated leadership. Long-term vision and strong management have long been absent from many European political circles, and coordination has suffered from the declining effectiveness and legitimacy of the EU institutions since the early 1990s. The successful introduction of the euro and the waves of enlargement masked this decline for a time, but the pitiful negotiations of December 2000 leading up to the Nice Treaty (which governs the EU today) made it clear that the EU was in serious trouble.

What could be called "the deconstruction of Europe" began in the early 1990s, following the difficult ratification debates surrounding the Maastricht Treaty and the official completion of the single market. The EU's intergovernmental institutions (mainly the European Council) took control of European unification at the expense of the European Commission and the European Court of Justice, which had been the twin boosters of European integration until then. The European Council committed itself to enlargement as the least controversial post-Cold War policy, but it proved incapable of strengthening EU institutions in a way that would preserve the cohesion and effectiveness of an expanding union. Without effective leadership from Brussels, the 15 western European member states diverged significantly in their economic and social policies and practices -- not to mention their visions of the EU itself. And the EU's eastward expansion, which brought union membership to 25 in 2004, was carried out without institutional reform, a sufficient financial commitment, or popular consultation and support.

Last spring, in rejecting the constitution, French and Dutch voters protested both the EU's poor economic record and its failure to maintain the sense of direction, homogeneity, identity, common purpose, and effectiveness that had carried the European project in its earlier years, however indeterminate the project may have been. These existential issues date back to the beginning of European unification, but the impact of successive waves of enlargement and the prospect of further expansion have made them impossible for Europeans to ignore. Despite the creation of a single market and the euro, the EU has not fulfilled its economic promise, even though economics is its undisputed domain, and the growing differences among its increasingly numerous members have tarnished the dream of its political unity. It was this twofold disappointment -- the crisis of performance and the crisis of identity -- rather than the fear of excessive integration that alienated a critical component of the French, Dutch, and other national electorates from the European project.

STUMBLING BLOCKS

Still, the troubles of the European constitution may be serving an important, if unintended, purpose: to challenge the conventional celebration of the European social model, which is often brandished to counter attempts to introduce structural reform in key member states. Even the French, who have long defended a "social Europe" against Anglo-Saxon economic liberalism and the newly emerging "barbarians" from Asia, can no longer convincingly claim that a system that produces massive, long-term unemployment and minimal growth is a model worth following. The post-referendum debate in France has finally acknowledged the diversity of Europe's economic and social practices and the difference between those states that have successfully adapted the welfare state and its ideology to market economics and global competition and those that have not. The United Kingdom, Ireland, Spain, and the Scandinavian and eastern European countries are doing well; the interventionist and socially rigid economies of Germany, France, and Italy are depressing EU growth and employment levels. The U.S. model remains anathema in Paris, but the combination of labor-market flexibility and social protection practiced in Scandinavia has become fashionable; in view of the United Kingdom's growth and employment records, even the "British model" is no longer taboo by the Seine.

With the United Kingdom assuming the EU's presidency for the second half of 2005, British Prime Minister Tony Blair has had an opportunity to invoke the French and Dutch votes and the budget deadlock to start a sound discussion on the EU's condition, question its current budget priorities, and call for modernizing the union to confront the challenges of the twenty-first century. Blair's address to the European Parliament on June 23, 2005 (in support of refocusing Europe's priorities toward growth, higher education, and research and innovation), may have been opportunistic, but it nonetheless received unexpected attention throughout the continent, including in Paris. Much as several years of economic and political stagnation precipitated the single-market program in the mid-1980s, the recent constitutional drama may have a positive aftermath and lead to a pragmatic rethinking of the EU's priorities.

One should not, however, underestimate the obstacles ahead. First among these are EU citizens' growing disenchantment with "Europe" and the troublesome mix of left-wing radicalism, right-wing sovereigntism, bipartisan populism, and anti-Americanism that buttressed the no votes. Despite their differences, these movements share a common aversion to market economics, economic competition, political liberalism, open borders, and transatlantic cooperation -- that is, to a good part of what the EU stands for and needs more of. Although at bottom the no votes were a cry for significant change, the immediate effect of the referendums will likely be a defense of national interests and social privileges, however illusory. National governments will have to navigate around this contradiction. In the short run, they will probably try to improve their economic and social records with mild liberal reforms while maintaining the good old rhetoric (and much of the reality) of the status quo. Going forward, political debates will likely pit a bolder embrace of liberal market economics against a more radically social and nationalist approach to economic and social ills. The latter is already gaining ground in France.

Already lacking at the national level, where it most matters, the political leadership required for change is unlikely to come from Brussels. Setbacks to the European unification process have typically been followed by extended freezes on EU initiatives. (The difficult Maastricht ratification debate altered the whole European dynamic of the second half of the 1980s.) As long as salvaging the constitutional treaty in one form or another remains a hope, the European Commission is unlikely to undertake any measure that might upset public opinion or a national government.

As could be expected, the British presidency of the EU has been too short and the challenge too formidable for the vision laid out in Blair's post-referendum agenda to have produced concrete results yet. In addition, France's irrational blow to its own vision of Europe as a world power has made the United Kingdom's influence within the EU both greater and more politically sensitive. Although the derailment of the constitutional project was a self-inflicted wound, it is widely viewed in continental Europe as the triumph of the Anglo-Saxon ambition for the EU: a vast free-trade area or, more plausibly, a loose confederation of nations cooperating on economic and certain political matters. The frustration many Europeans feel with such an outcome after 50 years of continuing unification will have to be addressed before a consensus on the European project can be rebuilt. And so even though the EU's substantive problems now appear more clearly to political leaders and public opinion, Europe is unlikely to be in a better position to deal with them for some time.

COLLATERAL DAMAGE

Despite the views of those who still believe that a weak and fragmented EU is a good thing for the United States, the present state of affairs should be a matter of concern for Washington. Thanks to the constitutional fiasco, pragmatism and economic reform now top the EU agenda, but opportunities for reform may still succumb to the political and ideological forces that sealed the constitution's fate. In the meantime, the political consequences of the no votes will undoubtedly be negative for the United States.

first and most important, Washington will have to wait longer for the EU to become the more effective partner that it and the rest of the world need. Although the constitutional treaty anticipated only modest steps in that direction -- such as a more stable EU presidency, an EU foreign minister, and certain improvements on security and defense -- even these are now on hold, as the EU can be expected to devote a considerable amount of time and energy to its internal problems rather than to world affairs. Europeans seem to want the EU to play a bigger role on the world scene, but that desire has not translated into more defense spending, a more consensual foreign policy, or a more strategic view of EU enlargement.

Even if dealing with a weakened, self-centered Europe would improve transatlantic relations (which remains to be seen), the United States needs more than that from a key ally in confronting global security and economic challenges. Without meaningful support from its European partners, Washington is likely to ignore them, fueling U.S. unilateralism, European resentment, and the tensions that have been so harmful in the past few years. Ad hoc groups set up to deal with discrete foreign policy and security matters, such as the European troika currently in talks over Iran's nuclear program, are useful second bests, but they are not nearly as effective as a stable and united global player allied with the United States.

The future of the EU's enlargement policy should be another, and perhaps more immediate, matter of concern for Washington. Among other things, the constitutional treaty's rejection by the French and the Dutch was a vote protesting the EU's admission, without popular consultation, of ten new members last year. For the treaty's opponents, as well as for many other Europeans, the EU's recent eastern enlargement poses two problems. First, the new members' more market-oriented (and more successful) economies raise fears of outsourcing, in addition to fears of increased competition in trade and from cheap immigrant labor. Second, the failure of the 15-member EU to strengthen its institutional system and rejuvenate its core mission has made the public fear, not without reason, that the 25-member union of today is an unworkable and unreasonable project.

These two sets of concerns are exacerbated by the prospect of Turkish membership, which also raises cultural, religious, and geopolitical issues for EU citizens. Indeed, the constitutional referendums have both turned enlargement into such a sensitive matter that national governments will no longer be able to bypass public opinion on it and put Turkey's membership, however distant, in even greater jeopardy than before. In a vain effort to insulate the constitutional referendum from popular fears relating to Turkey's possible accession, the French government imprudently amended the national constitution to require that, after Bulgaria and Romania join the EU, any further enlargement will have to be approved by referendum. That requirement is more likely to be imitated by other member states than ignored, casting doubt on any future expansion, including toward the Balkans.

Since the beginning of European unification, the United States has consistently advocated a wide and open union. European supporters of political integration regularly suspect that Washington's (and London's) pro-enlargement policy is motivated by the desire to prevent the advent of a more politically cohesive Europe. A more balanced assessment would stress that the United States has always had a primarily geopolitical vision of the European enterprise, regarding as its essential mission the spread of peace, democracy, and prosperity throughout and around Europe through the reinforcement of market mechanisms and the rule of law rather than through the creation of a United States of Europe. As it turns out, Europe has been remarkably successful at fulfilling the United States' hopes, and the EU's expansion toward southern and eastern Europe has been essential to regional prosperity and world stability. But the foreign policy virtues of expansion may now be reaching their limits: the enlarged EU is increasingly ineffective, and its citizens long for definite and politically meaningful borders and are widely opposed to Turkey's accession. During the negotiations between Brussels and Ankara, Washington should take greater account of the EU's sensitivities than it has in the past but still encourage institutional arrangements that preserve a close link between Turkey and the EU as well as, down the road, the prospect of membership for the Balkan countries.

The worst outcome of the EU's current crisis would be the gradual undoing of European unification, including in economic and trade matters, as a result of declining EU legitimacy and rising nationalism. Such a development would generate political instability and tensions in and around Europe, a concern that Washington has been spared for several decades. Although such a scenario appears unlikely, the persistence and rise of radical, nationalist, and anti-American tendencies in Europe is almost a certainty.

THE WAY FORWARD

So where does the EU go from here? There are no obvious legal or institutional solutions to the current impasse. The constitutional treaty itself, for which the ratification process continues, is bound to produce an unprecedented legal deadlock. Since the French and the Dutch voted against the document last spring and the referendum was postponed in the United Kingdom, other states, including Luxembourg, have ratified the treaty. The number of ratifying states now exceeds a majority of EU members and represents a majority of the EU's population. Still, unless the countries that rejected the constitution are invited to vote again on the same text (which is unlikely) or an amended version is submitted for ratification in all 25 members, the treaty is already history. In any event, not much will happen on this question (or any other) unless the winner of the French presidential elections, scheduled for the spring of 2007, is committed to putting France back in the EU driver's seat. Meanwhile, hopes that a strong Franco-German union or a union of core member states could counteract the EU's institutional weaknesses have become less realistic than ever in the aftermath of the French (and, to a lesser extent, the Dutch) vote, as both scenarios rely on a healthy France committed to a politically unified Europe and a Germany willing to permanently favor Paris over London or Washington. Although long-standing Euroskeptics such as Czech President Václav Klaus believe that the EU's current condition is a realistic, stable, and desirable outcome of a half century of European unification, most Europeans reject this view -- and with reason. The current state of the union, were it to last, would soon give way to the EU's regression.

In the end, only pragmatic steps can help the EU out of its crisis. The first one is to boost Europe's overall economic performance, improve its employment record, and ease its social malaise. This is largely a domestic challenge facing France, Germany, Italy, and other founding members. At the EU level, a few changes would be beneficial: realigning Germany and France along more liberal economic tracks and renewing the EU's commitment to both integration and its partnership with the

United States. These steps, both significant departures from the past few years, would strengthen European unity and in turn create an environment more favorable to a new European initiative to which the United Kingdom and eastern European members could subscribe. Further progress on institutional and policy matters (such as security and immigration policies) would also help reconcile the citizens of the former European Community with the enlarged EU. This is a key challenge, but it is also a prerequisite for future accessions, including those of Romania, Bulgaria, and the Balkan states. As for other countries, Brussels will have to devise a new form of economic and political partnership that falls short of actual membership.

All of these adjustments will require vision, leadership, and diplomacy on the part of European governments. It is ironic that the EU stumbled just as the Bush administration was beginning to acknowledge its existence and even its virtues. Still, Washington should help its European allies out of the impasse, if only to protect one of the key pillars of Western identity and global stability -- and the most progressive political experiment of our time.

LAURENT COHEN-TANUGI is a partner in the Paris office of Skadden, Arps, Slate, Meagher & Flom and the author of "An Alliance at Risk: The United States and Europe Since September 11."

March 12, 2009

Letter From London: One Market, Many Peoples

Will the Crash Scuttle the European Project?

Jeremy Shapiro

Anger against foreigners in Shepherd's Bush, my slightly seedy neighborhood of West London, is not hard to find. A late-night visit to a convenience store or a kebab shop often presents the spectacle of angry natives -- usually drunk and probably unemployed -- cursing at the lack of fellow countrymen working in the neighborhood. Their language is crude, but their analysis is hard to dispute: the store on my corner has Poles behind the cash registers and Pakistanis sweeping the floors.

Such workers are increasingly becoming targets for xenophobic wrath in the United Kingdom. The ongoing global economic crisis has hit the British employment market hard, with 278,000 native-born workers losing their jobs in the last year. At the same time, jobs for foreign-born workers rose by 214,000, and immigrants now represent nearly 15 percent of all workers in the United Kingdom. Many sectors, particularly the very visible construction trade, are dominated by foreign labor. This January, the revelation that the builders of a refinery in Lincolnshire had refused to consider British workers, instead hiring only Italian and Portuguese applicants, spawned a wave of wildcat refinery strikes across the country and blockades of power stations by outraged British energy workers. The famously anti-European British tabloid press decries the invasion of foreign labor and insists that Prime Minister Gordon Brown make good on his 2007 promise to find "British jobs for every British worker," even if that means reserving jobs for British workers.

Blaming foreigners for hard economic times is hardly a new phenomenon, even in ultra-cosmopolitan London. The United Kingdom, like much of Europe, has a long tradition of importing workers during good times and then struggling to respond to popular demands to send them home during downturns. This current recession, however, offers an additional complication: the single European labor market. A series of EU rules that have slowly come into place over the last 20 years now mean that the national governments of EU member states cannot make laws that discriminate against workers from other EU countries. Back in 2004, when ten countries (including eight from Eastern Europe) joined the EU, existing member states had the option of taking up to seven years to adopt a nondiscrimination policy against workers from the new member states. But Britain as well as Ireland and Sweden -- which all faced domestic labor shortages at the time -- chose to accept laborers from those countries immediately. Now there is no going back. During the boom years, workers from Eastern Europe, who were barred from countries such as Italy, France, and Germany, flocked to London, and many still continue to follow their friends and relatives to the United Kingdom. The result is that a neighborhood such as Shepherd's Bush is now a good place to find Polish delicacies and a bad place to find a plumber fluent in English.

Unlike the United Kingdom, most other EU countries have opened very slowly to labor from the East and thus do not yet have many intra-EU migrants in their labor forces, making the situation in the United Kingdom fairly specific. In most other EU countries, rage toward immigrants remains focused on workers who come from outside the EU -- Turkish guest workers in Germany, for example, or North African immigrants in France -- against whom national politicians are relatively free to discriminate.

The dilemma facing the United Kingdom does, however, parallel similar problems that other EU countries are having with the rules of the common market. The national governments of France and Italy, for instance, want to channel state subsidies to support national companies in strategic industries, a serious challenge to EU competition rules. In six EU countries -- Ireland, France, Greece, Latvia, Malta, and Spain -- national governments breached EU rules by allowing their budget deficits to exceed three percent of GDP, the limit set as part of the movement toward a single European currency. The European Commission is instituting legal proceedings against five of them, and it forecasts that by next year 16 of the 27 member states will exceed the limit. Across the EU, governments are trying to insert "buy national" provisions into their bank and industrial bailouts or simply urging consumers to "buy local." Although such actions violate the spirit and often the letter of common market rules, they are a necessary political concession to assure constituents that their tax money won't be spent creating jobs in other EU countries.

This resistance to EU common-market rules is evidence of a deeper problem -- namely, the absence of a European identity. New Yorkers do not complain that workers from Michigan are taking their jobs or driving down their wages. But many Londoners and Parisians view Polish plumbers as a foreign threat to national prosperity.

The EU has tried for decades to create a sense of continental solidarity that might underpin the single European market in hard times. It now has a flag, an anthem, and a celebrated new Internet domain (.eu). In 2005, European leaders even attempted to establish a constitution. But as the decisive rejection of the constitution in referendums in France and the Netherlands showed -- and as seen in reactions to the economic downturn throughout Europe -- bureaucrats in Brussels have not managed to create much of a sense of European identity. For the most part, European public opinion remains resolutely national in its outlook.

Europe, then, has a single market without a single identity, which means that people who feel little communal tie to one another are now legally bound together in a seamless economic community. This situation creates a political paradox, which in a serious recession, acts to constrain leaders such as Gordon Brown, who faces calls from the British public to protect it against foreign threats but is no longer legally allowed even to acknowledge those threats as foreign, let alone satisfy the demands for protection. When a head of state does attempt to accommodate a frightened public -- such as when French President Nicolas Sarkozy suggested that French car companies would have to bring their factories back to France as a condition of an auto-industry bailout -- these efforts are quickly met with moralistic rebukes from other European states, public lectures from Brussels bureaucrats, and in some cases, legal proceedings from the European Commission.

Although EU rules may help to prevent counterproductive protectionism, one has to believe that, in the end, democratic politics will bend to popular will. In Britain, anger against migration is growing and, for the first time, is focusing more on intra-European migrant labor than on workers from former imperial domains. The resolutely Euro-skeptical Tory party is expected to win next year's general election, a prediction made more certain with each outburst of anger against European workers. If the economic downturn continues and the Tories do emerge victorious, they will probably use their mandate to call into question much of what the EU has built in recent years. In that case, many other European countries that are trying to cope with similar political dilemmas may follow the British lead in abandoning single-market restrictions. The greatest experiment in history of creating a single market larger than the nation-state may be at risk because it contains too many foreigners.

JEREMY SHAPIRO is Director of Research at the Center on the United States and Europe at the Brookings Institution.

Saving the Euro, Dividing the Union

Could Europe's Deeper Integration Push the United Kingdom Out?

R. Daniel kelemen

David Cameron arrives at an EU summit in Brussels.

In an article I wrote last May, I argued that Europe's future would be defined by a "new normal." The road to economic recovery would be long and painful, but thanks to aggressive intervention by the European Central Bank and the new continent-wide governance structures being put in place, the eurozone's collapse was no longer a serious risk. The credit ratings agencies now seem to agree. The year 2012 ended with Standard & Poor's upgrading its assessment of Greek sovereign debt. Last week, Fitch declared that the odds of a eurozone breakup are now "very unlikely." Although record unemployment persists in the periphery of the common currency area and growth prospects have dimmed for Germany and other core countries, there is a growing consensus that the worst may be over.

Instead of unraveling, as so many skeptics had predicted, European countries responded to the economic crisis by taking significant steps toward deepening their integration. The continent's leaders granted EU institutions greater control over the fiscal policy of member states, ratified a fiscal compact, and reached an agreement on the outlines of a banking union. European Central Bank President Mario Draghi emphasized the bank's commitment to do "whatever it takes" to save the common currency.

But this incremental deepening of European integration may come at a cost: Not all 27 member states want to be part of a closer union -- least of all the United Kingdom. Talk of a "Grexit" from the euro has been replaced by talk of "Brexit" -- a British exit -- from the European Union itself. Euroskepticism in the United Kingdom has reached historic heights. The U.K. Independence Party, which is committed to London's leaving the EU, has overtaken the Liberal Democrats as the third most popular party. Recent polls suggest that a majority of British residents favor an exit. British Prime Minister David Cameron, facing enormous pressure from Euroskeptic backbenchers in his own party, will soon deliver a major speech on the United Kingdom's relationship with the EU. He is likely to call for the repatriation of powers from the EU in areas such as social policy, employment, and justice, and promise a national referendum on a "new deal" with Europe. Meanwhile, many leaders on the continent are tiring of Cameron's anti-European rhetoric and his demands for special treatment and opt-outs.

As the EU takes steps to strengthen its economic and political union, it is likely to drive a deeper wedge between core eurozone states and member states outside of the common currency that are unwilling to go along. Officials in Brussels have suggested that tensions caused by tighter coordination in the common currency area can be addressed by developing new forms of what is known as two-speed or multi-speed integration, whereby core groups of countries move ahead with deeper union on certain policies, while others opt out. Although this flexible approach has worked in the past, including for the establishment of the eurozone itself, there are reasons to believe it may be less tenable today as the EU moves toward an unprecedentedly close economic, fiscal, and political union. Flexible, à la carte approaches will not by themselves resolve the tensions between the countries committed to deepening their union and those refusing to take part.

ORIGINAL ARTICLE: May 16, 2012

The eurozone's troubles no longer qualify as a crisis, an unstable situation that could either quickly improve or take a dramatic turn for the worse. They are, instead, a new normal - - a painful situation, to be sure, but one that will last for years to come. Citizens, investors, and policymakers should let go of the idea that there is some magic bullet that could quickly kill off Europe's ailments. By the same token, despite the real possibility of Greek exit, the eurozone is not on the brink of collapse. The European Union and its common currency will hold together, but the road to recovery will be long. It has been nearly two and a half years since the incoming socialist government in Greece revealed the extent to which its predecessor had accumulated debt, precipitating an economic storm that has left slashed budgets, collapsed governments, and record unemployment in its wake. With each dramatic turn, observers have anticipated the story's denouement. But again and again, a definitive resolution -- either a policy fix or a total collapse -- has failed to emerge.

The truth is that there are no quick escapes from the eurozone's predicament. Divorce is no solution. Although some economists suggest that struggling countries on the periphery could leave the euro and return to a national currency in order to regain competitiveness and restore growth, no country would willingly leave the eurozone; doing so would amount to economic suicide. Its financial system would collapse, and ensuing bank runs and riots would make today's social unrest seem quaint by comparison. What is more, even after a partial default, the country's government and financial firms would still be burdened by debt denominated largely in euros. As the value of the new national currency plummeted, the debt would become unbearable, and the government, now outside the club, would not be able to turn to the eurozone for help.

Some economists go further and argue that countries on Europe's periphery could thrive outside the euro straitjacket. This is equally unconvincing. Southern European countries' economies suffer from deep structural problems that predate the euro. Spanish unemployment rates fluctuated between 15 and 22 percent throughout most of the 1990s; Greece has been in default for nearly half of its history as an independent state. These countries are far more likely to tackle their underlying problems and thrive inside the eurozone than outside it.

Others have suggested that Germany and other core countries -- weary of funding endless bailouts -- might abandon the euro. That is even less plausible. Germany has been the greatest beneficiary of European integration and the common currency. Forty percent of German exports go to eurozone countries, and the common currency has reduced transaction costs and boosted German growth. An unraveling of the eurozone would devastate German banks, and any new German currency would appreciate rapidly, damaging the country's export-led economic model.

A number of policy reforms may improve economic conditions in the eurozone, but none offers a panacea. Eurobonds, increased investment in struggling economies through the European Investment Bank and other funds, stricter regulations of banks, a common deposit insurance system, a shift from budget cuts to structural reforms that enhance productivity and encourage private-sector job creation -- all of these could improve Europe's economic situation and should be implemented.

But none of these measures would quickly restore growth or bring employment back to pre-crisis levels. That is because they do not address Europe's central economic problem: the massive debt accumulated by the periphery countries during last decade's credit boom. The 2000s saw a tremendous amount of capital flow from the northern European countries to private- and public-sector borrowers in Greece, Ireland, Portugal, and Spain. Germany and other countries with current account surpluses flooded the periphery with easy credit, and the periphery gobbled it up. This boosted domestic demand and generated growth in the periphery but also encouraged wage inflation that undermined competitiveness and left massive debt behind. As the economists Carmen Reinhart and Kenneth Rogoff have pointed out, when countries suffer a recession caused by a financial crisis and debt overhang, they take many years to recover.

With both breakup and immediate solutions off the table, then, the eurozone is settling into a new normal. As the union slowly digs itself out of the economic pit, it is important to recognize that its system of economic governance has already been fundamentally transformed over the past two years.

First, the eurozone has, at least in practice, done away with its founding documents. In any monetary union in which states retain the autonomy to tax, spend, and borrow, there is a risk that some countries' excessive borrowing could threaten the value of the common currency. Recognizing this, the euro's creators drafted the Stability and Growth Pact and the "no bailout" clause in the Maastricht Treaty. The SGP placed legal restrictions on member-state deficit and debt levels, and the no-bailout clause forbade the European Union or individual member states from bailing out over-indebted states to avoid moral hazard.

The Maastricht governance regime is dead. The SGP was never strictly enforced, and when the crisis hit, the European Union tossed aside the no-bailout clause. Fearing contagion, it extended emergency loans to Greece, Ireland, and Portugal and set up a permanent bailout fund -- the European Stability Mechanism (ESM) -- which will be up and running this summer.

Having broken the taboo on bailouts, Europe had to find a way to limit the moral hazard of states turning again and again to the European Union for aid. EU lawmakers introduced the so-called six-pack legislation, which strengthened the European Commission's ability to monitor member states' fiscal policies and enforce debt limits. Twenty-five EU member states signed a fiscal compact treaty, which committed them to enshrining deficit limits into national law. Only those states that eventually ratify the treaty will be eligible for loans from the ESM.

Such legal provisions alone will not overcome the moral hazard, but they have been accompanied by evolution in bond markets, which now distinguish between the debt of healthy governments in the core and weak ones on the periphery. For the first decade of the euro's young life, bond markets priced the risk associated with the peripheral economies' bonds nearly the same as that associated with German ones. Today, the yield spreads are substantial and increase at the first sign of heightened risk. And by forcing private investors to take a nearly 75 percent loss on Greek bonds in conjunction with the second Greek bailout in February 2012, European leaders made clear that private bondholders should not expect bailouts to cover their losses, too. Now, more vigilant bond markets will police governments that run up unsustainable deficits or whose banking sectors grow fragile.

The second major structural change is that the European Central Bank -- legally prohibited from purchasing any member state's debt -- has thrown its rules aside and directly purchased billions in Greek, Irish, Italian, Portuguese, and Spanish bonds. Moreover, the ECB has indirectly financed billions more loans through its long-term refinancing operation, which extended over a trillion euros in low-interest loans to commercial banks.

ECB President Mario Draghi has repeatedly insisted that the bank is not engaging in "monetary financing" of member-state debts. If I were an Italian president of a central bank located in Frankfurt with a mandate designed by German inflation hawks, I would say that, too. But in practice, the ECB has shown itself to be far more flexible than many had anticipated. It has revealed, quite simply, that it will not oversee the demise of the currency that justifies its existence.

This new system of eurozone governance is more sustainable than the pre-crisis regime set in place by the Maastricht Treaty. It will withstand a Greek exit, for example. If Greece refuses to adhere to the terms of its bailout package and is forced out of the eurozone in the coming weeks, the ECB will likely scramble to stop contagion, but it will not be faced with the entire system's collapse. Meanwhile, by standing firm on Greece, the European Union will have further demonstrated that the conditions attached to its bailouts are serious, motivating other states to stick to their reform programs.

Greece's exit from the eurozone would be a catastrophe for Greece and a trauma for Europe, but it would not change the fundamentals of the post-2008 eurozone governance regime, which will still be based on stronger fiscal surveillance, more robust enforcement procedures, more vigilant bond markets, and a more activist central bank. With such a system in place, and with their commitment to fiscal discipline established, EU leaders will now face the slow, difficult tasks of adjustment and structural reform. And those burdens must be shared by all. It is understandable that Germany and the ECB initially demanded austerity as the condition for bailouts, but this one-sided approach has driven peripheral economies deeper into recession. Moving forward, austerity, wage reductions, and structural reform on the periphery must be coupled with public spending and wage increases in Germany, which will boost demand. There will be no quick fix, but the eurozone will recover, slowly but surely.

R. DANIEL KELEMEN is Professor of Political Science and Director of the Center for European Studies at Rutgers University. He is the author of *Eurolegalism: The Transformation of Law and Regulation in the European Union.*

© Foreign Affairs

The New British Politics

What the UKIP Victory and the Scottish Referendum Have in Common

Andrew Hammond

STEFAN WERMUTH / COURTESY REUTERS

Newly elected United Kingdom Independence Party MP Douglas Carswell arrives at Parliament, October 13, 2014.

It has been less than a month since the United Kingdom's domestic politics captured world headlines with the landmark Scottish referendum on independence. However, yet another (somewhat smaller) political earthquake rippled through the British electoral landscape on Friday with the news that the United Kingdom Independence Party (UKIP) has won its first seat in the House of Commons in Clacton, southern England.

UKIP, a party built around a policy of British withdrawal from the European Union, claims that the victory signals a "shift in the tectonic plates of British politics." And, indeed, it could be a precursor to another UKIP victory in the November 20 by-election in Strood and Rochester, which is also in southern England.

To be sure, some dismiss UKIP's success last Friday as an electoral flash in the pan. But that ignores the party's earlier success in May, when it won the European Parliament vote in the United Kingdom, thus becoming the first party other than the Conservatives or Labour to win a national election in more than 100 years.

UKIP's by-election victory and last month's Scottish referendum may seem unrelated. But they both reflect flux in British politics: a relatively stable two-party system is giving way to more unpredictability. For much of the postwar period, British politics has been dominated by the Conservatives and Labour. Between 1945 and 1970, for instance, the two parties collectively won an average of over 90 percent of the vote -- and seats -- in the eight British general elections held in that time.

Yet in the nine elections held between 1974 and 2005, that average fell significantly to below 75 percent. And that has brought about major political changes that are still unfolding to this day. The Liberals have done most in recent decades to break the hold of the two major parties on power. From 1974 to 2005, the average Liberal share of the vote (including an alliance between the Liberals and the United Kingdom's Social Democratic Party [SDP] from 1983 to 1987) in British general elections was just below 20 percent.

Although Liberals have long taken votes from both major parties, the Liberals' overall political impact on Labour has probably been most pronounced. The Liberals kept the party in power from 1977 to 1978 under the Lib-Lab pact, and pro-EU elements of the Labour Party worked with Liberals during the 1975 referendum on the United Kingdom's membership in the EU.

However, in 1981, following Labour's defeat to the Conservatives in the 1979 general election, the creation of the SDP (which would later that year form an alliance with the Liberals and ultimately become the Liberal Democrats we know today) shook the foundations of British politics. The SDP was founded by key Labour figures concerned by the growing power of the left within the party.

The Liberal-SDP alliance quickly won a number of by-elections and headed national polls for some time. Moreover, in the 1983 general election, the alliance won some 25 percent of the vote -- the best third party performance in the postwar era and only just behind the 27 percent recorded by Labour that year.

The success of the alliance was one factor that helped contribute to Labour's long period in opposition from 1979 to 1997, when it endured four consecutive general election defeats. Prior to 1997, Paddy Ashdown, then leader of the Liberal Democrats, and Tony Blair, then leader of Labour, had discussed the possibility of a formal government coalition to reunite the center-left vote in British politics. However, Labour won a massive majority in 1997 that made this prospect unnecessary.

Aside from the Liberals, several other parties have come to prominence in recent years, including the Scottish National Party (SNP), which governs in the Edinburgh Parliament; UKIP, whose strength lies largely in the United Kingdom; and the Greens. In recent weeks, opinion polls indicated that, collectively, these parties and the Liberal Democrats enjoy the support of around 30 percent of the electorate.

Recently, it is UKIP that has seen its fortunes rise, and this has caused particular problems for the Conservative Party. Driven in part by UKIP's appeal, which is disproportionately to Conservative rather than Labour voters, Prime Minister David Cameron has promised that if he wins a majority in the 2015 general election, by 2017, he will hold an "in or out" referendum on the EU. As the recent European Parliament elections underlined, such a plebiscite could well see the United Kingdom vote to leave.

As the two-party system has declined, British politics has become more uncertain, because it is harder for any one group to secure a majority in general elections. This is despite first-past-the-post voting, which tends to provide the leading party with a significantly larger number of seats in the House of Commons than would be given by a more proportionate electoral system.

It is hard to overstate the importance of the shift. Until 2010, when the current coalition government was formed between the Liberal Democrats and the Conservatives, Labour and the Conservatives had won overall majority governments at every election since 1945, except for a brief interregnum between February and October 1974.

Yet, as in 2010, the precise result of the May 2015 British general election is once more unpredictable. While Labour has enjoyed a poll lead in most surveys since 2010, a number of polls this month show the Conservatives with a slight advantage.

To be sure, Labour or possibly the Conservatives could yet win an overall majority. However, the conditions look good for another hung Parliament, in which no one party wins a majority of seats.

Another hung Parliament could mean a second successive coalition government, possibly this time among more than two parties. A second possibility is the prospect of either Labour or the Conservatives seeking to run a minority government without a parliamentary majority, over a five-year term of office, with all the uncertainties this might bring.

A minority government could potentially function through a "confidence and supply" arrangement, in which a party agrees to support the government in motions of confidence and potentially appropriation votes by voting in favor or abstaining. Last week, UKIP leader Nigel Farage said that his political price for supporting the Conservatives in this way would be the early staging of an EU referendum in July 2015, before Parliament's summer recess.

If there is a hung Parliament in next year's election, it is likely that the precise parliamentary arithmetic would help decide whether there is a coalition or minority government. The closer any party gets to 326 of the total 650 seats, the more likely a minority administration may become.

In October 1974, for instance, Labour won the general election, but over time, its majority eroded. In 1977, with a now minority government, Prime Minister Jim Callaghan negotiated the Lib-Lab pact, which secured the parliamentary support of Liberal parliamentarians on votes of no confidence. This sustained the government for nearly a year and a half, until the pact came to an end in 1978, during a period when Labour was facing significant opposition, including intraparty, to public spending reductions to help pay for the 1976 International Monetary Fund loan.

Taken as a whole, the rise of parties such as UKIP and the SNP underlines the United Kingdom's postwar political system is giving way, in the medium term, at least, to a more unpredictable and uncertain British political landscape. Indeed, barring a significant polling surge by Labour or the Conservatives, a second successive British hung Parliament looks increasingly possible with the intensified political uncertainties this may bring.

ANDREW HAMMOND is an Associate at LSE IDEAS at the London School of Economics. He was formerly a UK Government Special Adviser.

© Foreign Affairs

Littler England

The United Kingdom's Retreat From Global Leadership

Anand Menon

A member of the Scots Guards receives his duties during the daily Changing of the Guard ceremony at Buckingham Palace in London, April, 2011.

In the last year, some 39,000 migrants, mostly from North Africa, tried to make their way to the United Kingdom from the French port of Calais by boarding trucks and trains crossing the English Channel. In response, the British government attempted to secure the entrance to thetunnel in Calais, dispatching two and a half miles of security fencing that had been used for the 2012 Olympics and the 2014 NATO summit.

The United Kingdom's improvised response to the migrant crisis, with recycled fences substituting for a coherent immigration policy, is emblematic of its increasingly parochial approach to the world beyond its shores. The Conservative government of Prime Minister David Cameron appears to lack a clear vision of the country's place on the global stage. The United Kingdom, a nuclear power and permanent member of the UN Security Council, now seems intent not on engaging with the outside world but on insulating itself from it. The United Kingdom does not merely lack a grand strategy. It lacks any kind of clearly defined foreign policy at all, beyond a narrow trade agenda.

Historically, the United Kingdom has been an active player in world politics. After the loss of its empire, the country was a founding and engaged member of the institutions of the postwar Western order. British governments have led the way in pressing for, and undertaking, humanitarian interventions from Sierra Leone to Kosovo. And the United Kingdom's relationship with the United States has been a great asset to both sides since World War II.

Recently, however, factors including fatigue following the wars in Afghanistan and Iraq, a recession, and a prime minister with little apparent interest in foreign affairs have conspired to render the British increasingly insular. The British diplomatic corps and military have seen their capabilities slashed amid harsh austerity measures. In its limited contribution to the campaign against the self-proclaimed Islamic State (also known as ISIS), in its mercantilist approach to China, and in its inability to formulate a real strategy to respond to Russia's aggression in Ukraine, the United Kingdom has prioritized narrow economic interests to the detriment of broader considerations of international security.

With a national referendum on the United Kingdom's EU membership likely to be held in 2016, debates about the country's place in the world will come into sharper focus. What exactly is the United Kingdom capable of achieving when acting alone? Should London work with partners to compensate for declining national capabilities? Do international organizations increase or constrain the power and influence of their member states?

The answers the United Kingdom provides to these questions will shape its engagement with international politics in the years to come. A vote in favor of a British exit would embroil London and Brussels in months of bitter argument, heightening already disturbingly high levels of European parochialism. It would weaken not only the United Kingdom but also the EU, deprived of its most globally engaged and militarily powerful member state.

TIGHTENED PURSE STRINGS

Budget cuts are the most visible sign of the United Kingdom's retreat. The budget of the Foreign Office has been cut by 20 percent since 2010, and the ministry has been told to prepare for further reductions of 25 to 40 percent. The armed forces have also been downsized, with the army alone expected to shrink from 102,000 soldiers in

2010 to 82,000 by 2020. The former head of the Royal Navy has spoken of "uncomfortable similarities" between the United Kingdom's defenses now and those in the early 1930s.

The United Kingdom does not merely lack a grand strategy. It lacks any kind of clearly defined foreign policy at all

So much have British capabilities declined that during NATO's 2011 mission in Libya, the United Kingdom was painfully dependent on U.S. support to fight a third-rate military. In the current campaign against the Islamic State, a shortage of already antiquated Tornado ground attack jets has kept the British contribution to the air strikes limited, with only eight aircraft being deployed. And the United Kingdom's decision to scrap its Nimrod maritime surveillance aircraft in 2010 has left the country vulnerable to the incursion of Russian submarines in the Irish Sea.

The penchant for disengagement has not been confined to the executive branch. In 2013, the British Parliament voted against intervention in Syria, presaging a more cautious approach to military intervention in general. Public opinion seems equally allergic to foreign entanglements. A 2015 Pew poll found that less than half of the British public favors using force to defend the territory of a NATO ally that falls victim to armed aggression. It was hardly inaccurate for the foreign secretary, Philip Hammond, to declare, in the run-up to the 2015 election, that "there are no votes in defense." Meanwhile, the opposition Labour Party has elected a leader, Jeremy Corbyn, who is opposed to all military intervention unless explicit UN approval is secured, who has compared atrocities committed by the Islamic State to U.S. actions in Fallujah, and who has called for British withdrawal from NATO.

FOLLOW THE MONEY

As British policymakers have lost interest in engaging with the outside world, they have embraced a shortsighted conception of economic interests. The Foreign Office has had its ambitions lowered, with its main role now to promote trade as part of the government's so-called prosperity agenda.

This narrow focus can be seen most clearly in China, where the British government has pursued political appeasement for economic gain. In July, the United Kingdom initially refused to grant a visa to the Chinese dissident artist Ai Weiwei, which many saw as an attempt to curry favor with Chinese President Xi Jinping before his visit to London in October. Although most parts of the Foreign Office have faced severe cuts in staff, the British embassy in Beijing has become bloated with commercial employees.

Russian oligarchs seeking property in London continue to receive a warm welcome, despite their support for Russian President Vladimir Putin.

Observers could be forgiven for thinking that the notion that China may pose a geopolitical challenge has not occurred to the British foreign policy establishment. On his recent trip to Indonesia, Malaysia, Singapore, and Vietnam, Cameron said next to nothing about the security concerns troubling that region, but he did oversee the signing of several trade deals.

Such mercantilist priorities are also shaping British foreign policy in the Persian Gulf, where, for instance, the pursuit of lucrative arms contracts with Bahrain has come to supersede strategic considerations of regional stability or the promotion of democracy. A similar myopia defines the British response to Russia. Almost a decade since the former Russian spy Alexander Litvinenko was murdered in London, most likely by Russian agents, there is still no sign of a coherent British approach to Russian aggression beyond the occasional firm word. The United Kingdom has been content to leave it up to France and Germany to lead the European diplomatic response to the Ukrainian crisis. And Russian oligarchs seeking property in London continue to receive a warm welcome, despite their support for Russian President Vladimir Putin.

What is so confounding about London's narrow mercantilism is that even if economic prosperity were the chief objective of foreign policy, the current approach would still be shortsighted. Profitable trade depends on the preservation of a stable and rule-bound international system, which both the Islamic State and Putin seek to revise. China may be a large and enticing market, but geopolitical rivalry in Asia represents a real threat to global prosperity. An emphasis on trade policy alone will do nothing to address major challenges to the international order, including piracy off the coast of Africa, the Islamic State's attempts to throw the economies of the Middle East and North Africa into turmoil, and the massive flow of migrants across the Mediterranean. No European state—indeed, no state at all—can hope to confront these challenges alone. For a country with limited means, dealing with problems of this scale requires collective action.

IN OR OUT?

Yet precisely when international cooperation is needed most, a new political argument threatens to weaken the United Kingdom's ability to collaborate: the debate over whether the country should leave the EU. Cameron has promised a referendum on EU membership by the end of 2017, and it appears likely that one will take place in 2016. The United Kingdom—like all EU members—continues to pursue its own foreign policy alongside those formulated for the EU as a whole in Brussels. If, however, it votes to leave the union, it will weaken its global influence and further jeopardize the stability of the international order.

For some proponents of a British exit from the EU, or "Brexit," withdrawal forms part of a broader strategy of retrenchment. Twenty-four of the 30 Conservative members of Parliament who voted against intervention in Syria also defied their own party to vote in favor of a referendum on EU membership in October 2011.

For other Euroskeptics, however, a British exit offers a way of reinforcing the United Kingdom's global heft. Nigel Farage, the leader of the right-wing UK

Independence Party, has held out the vision of the United Kingdom outside the EU as a "thriving, energetic, global hub."

The clunky, bureaucratic EU, these Euroskeptics argue, lacks the agility to pursue the kind of nimble foreign policy that a globalized world increasingly demands. Besides, they point out, the economic benefits of continued membership are small. Almost 60 percent of British exports currently go to countries outside the EU, so it makes little sense for so much of the British economy to be bound by the EU's strict regulations. And for those worried about geopolitical challenges, a United Kingdom that left the EU would still have its security guaranteed by its membership in NATO.

Many of the criticisms of the EU as a forum for foreign policy collaboration are accurate. More than 20 years of trying to create what the EU terms a "common foreign and security policy" has led to countless summits, declarations, targets, and rhetoric, but precious little in the way of substantive policies. There is little meaningful European defense collaboration, nor is there a robust common policy toward China. And when it comes to confronting insecurity in its own backyard—whether to the south or the east—the EU has strategies aplenty but few effective policies.

YVES HERMAN / REUTERS

Britain's Prime Minister David Cameron (L) meets with China's President Xi Jinping in The Hague, March, 2014.

Yet the Euroskeptics are wrong to ascribe all the blame for these failings to the much-maligned bureaucrats in Brussels. A lot of the fault lies with the member states themselves, who have refused to commit themselves wholeheartedly to a multilateral

European foreign policy. But since the capabilities of even large EU members, such as the United Kingdom, are declining, they have little choice but to invest in an imperfect institution.

Only the EU possesses structures to foster cooperation on everything from trade policy to sanctions to the defense industry. In a complex world, economic and security problems are intricately intertwined, and only a comprehensive approach to them has any chance of success. A more genuine commitment to such multilateralism from key member states, such as the United Kingdom, is essential to ensure that institutional inadequacies in Brussels are successfully addressed and overcome.

FORTRESS BRITAIN?

Buried within some of the Euroskeptics' criticisms of EU membership lies a paradox about British power. On the one hand, advocates of Brexit argue that London is too weak to wield sufficient influence in Brussels. They contend that the EU's excessive regulation and internal empire building—epitomized by its drive toward "an ever-closer union"—are long-term trends that the United Kingdom can do little or nothing to stymie. On the other hand, the skeptics maintain that the United Kingdom is so inherently powerful that free from the shackles of the EU, it would suddenly enjoy enough global heft to negotiate trade deals effectively with the likes of China.

The evidence suggests that, at least when it comes to China, London has limited influence. In May 2012, during his first term, Cameron met with the Dalai Lama, provoking Chinese criticism, before changing course and voicing opposition to Tibetan independence the following year. Yet neither move engendered any perceptible change in Chinese policy. Nor is there any credible evidence that London's pandering to Beijing was the reason China invested twice as much in the United Kingdom between 2012 and 2014 as it had in the previous seven years.

A migrant stands along a security fence topped with barbed and razor wire near the makeshift camp called "The New Jungle" in Calais, France, September, 2015.

Even if the United Kingdom were able to strike an advantageous trade deal with China by leaving the EU, it would be forgoing far more important benefits of EU membership. For one thing, trade is not merely about trade. The Transatlantic Trade and Investment Partnership, currently under negotiation between Brussels and Washington, could provide significant economic benefits (primarily from the removal of nontariff barriers, as tariffs between the United States and Europe are already low). Yet its implications are geopolitical as much as economic. The deal is as much about underlining the solidarity of the nations of the Western Hemisphere in the face of common political challenges as it is about eking out marginal gains from opening trade still further.

And this solidarity is crucial in today's unstable world. The United Kingdom cannot defend its interests alone. Many proponents of Brexit argue that international collaboration should occur with the United States rather than through the EU. Yet it's not clear that U.S. policymakers are interested in working with an insular United Kingdom adrift from the EU. British timidity feeds U.S. disenchantment with the United Kingdom by contributing to the perception that the country is disengaging not only from Europe but also from the wider world and that it is willing to sacrifice geopolitical principles in the name of prosperity. The United Kingdom's absence from the Minsk talks over the crisis in Ukraine and from unstable regions such as the Sahel—precisely where the United States is looking to Europeans to pick up the slack as it pivots toward Asia—reinforces such doubts across the Atlantic.

olidarity is crucial in today's *unstable world. The United Kingdom cannot defend its interests alone.*

These days, Washington is longing for its allies to take on a greater share of the burden of maintaining security in their own backyards. Moreover, and in stark contrast to earlier periods, Washington has increasingly come to believe that for the Europeans to be able to maintain security, they will need to work together within the EU. No longer does Europe stand in opposition to the transatlantic relationship; it now represents one of its building blocks. The route to a more effective NATO runs through central Brussels. It is precisely by using EU structures that Europeans can best facilitate the military collaboration that is required to strengthen the transatlantic alliance.

A MORE PERFECT UNION

It is difficult to exaggerate the difference the United Kingdom could make if it decided to throw itself wholeheartedly into the work of building collective foreign and security policies. On the rare occasions when London opts for such engagement—as it has with the EU's mission to combat piracy off the coast of Africa, for example—collective action proves enormously effective. But when it remains diffident about taking the lead in the EU, it not only weakens the EU but also creates a self-fulfilling prophecy: by contributing to the EU's ineffectiveness, British reluctance to provide leadership serves only to strengthen the arguments for Brexit.

As one of Europe's strongest military powers, the United Kingdom is well placed to lead. It was Tony Blair's government that finally allowed the EU, tentatively, to begin to formulate its own defense policies. And it was subsequent British diffidence that contributed to those policies' increasing ineffectiveness. By taking the lead when it comes to collaboration over weapons programs, by engaging fully in discussions over how to implement European military interventions, and by actively helping shape the union's foreign policies, London could arguably do more than any of its partners to reinforce Europe's international influence.

Uncertainty about the United Kingdom's place in the world is hardly a new phenomenon. In 1962, former U.S. Secretary of State Dean Acheson declared, "Great Britain has lost an empire and has not yet found a role." Today, the United Kingdom exhibits an even greater reluctance to engage in international affairs. The upcoming referendum will determine whether the country's retreat will continue unchecked. Yet whether it wishes to or not, the United Kingdom cannot detach itself entirely from events in eastern Europe, the Middle East, or Asia. Collective European action, of precisely the kind the EU was designed to foster, represents the only viable alternative.

ANAND MENON is Professor of European Politics and Foreign Affairs at King's College London. Follow him on Twitter @anandmenon1.
© Foreign Affairs

Should It Stay or Should It Go?

The Brexistential Crisis

R. Daniel Kelemen and Matthias Matthijs

Britain's UKIP party leader Nigel Farage holds his passport during his keynote address at the party's spring conference, in Llandudno, Britain February 27, 2016.

British Prime Minister David Cameron was quick to claim victory after the recent European Council meeting on the United Kingdom's relationship with the European Union. After marathon talks that saw Cameron and his team sustain themselves on 23 bags of Haribo gummy sweets and a famished German Chancellor Angela Merkel forced to pop around the corner for some Belgian Frites with mayonnaise, the United Kingdom and its European partners finally reached an agreement. As Cameron put it, he had obtained a "special status" for his country and could now campaign with all his "heart and soul" for Britain to remain in the European Union, thus avoiding a Brexit (or British exit).

The reforms agreed to last week are mostly inconsequential, but the negotiations between the United Kingdom and its EU partners were never about substance. The summit was largely a charade organized for British domestic consumption. Against the odds, Cameron's Conservative government swept to power last year pledging to negotiate "a new settlement for Britain in Europe" before holding a referendum on whether the United Kingdom should remain a member of the European Union. Cameron hoped that on the basis of this new deal, most Conservative Members of Parliament would join him in supporting the "in" campaign. Ultimately, Cameron wants the British people to vote to keep his country in the Union. Thus the political theater surrounding the summit last week was designed to enable Cameron to claim that he hadfought tooth-and-nail for British interests and won significant concessions from the European Union—even if the reforms do not amount to much in practice. With the renegotiations finally completed, the real battle has now begun in earnest.

A DATE WITH DESTINY

Cameron has set the date of the EU referendum: Thursday, June 23, 2016. The vote is less than four months away, and rival campaigns—one side for continued membership in the Union, the other favoring a Brexit—have hit the ground running. The looming referendum quickly exposed a sharp division within Cameron's own Conservative government, with six ministers announcing that they would back a Brexit. Among these, Justice Secretary Michael Gove, one of Cameron's closest political allies, is perhaps the most consequential, as he will add intellectual heft to the Brexit campaign. London's popular, flamboyant Mayor Boris Johnson has also announced he would join the "outs" adding mainstream star-power to a coalition that is otherwise comprised of octogenarian Thatcherites like former grandees Nigel Lawson andNorman Tebbit, and fringe figures from the United Kingdom Independence Party (UKIP), led by Nigel Farage. In all, about half of theConservative Members of Parliament are likely to actively campaign for Britain to leave the European Union.

But in the end, it will be the British people—rather than the politicians—who decide. Their choice will have profound consequences for the future of the United Kingdom and Europe. If the British people file for divorce on June 23, the United Kingdom will regain some autonomy in policymaking, although much less than Brexit campaigners have promised. This newfound independence, however, could come at a very high price. Brexit would destabilize a European Union that is already plagued by multiple crises, create chaos across international financial markets, damage the British economy, and could even lead to the dissolution of the United Kingdom itself if the Scottish National Party(SNP) makes good on its promise of holding a second referendum on Scotland's independence if the United Kingdom votes to leave the European Union.

THE NOT-SO-NEW DEAL

The United Kingdom's "New Settlement" with the European Union targets four areas: competitiveness, economic governance, sovereignty, and migration. Most of the reforms were either purely symbolic or marginal changes that largely reaffirm existing policies. The reforms concerning benefits for migrants do address a core concern of Brexit supporters, but even on this issue the substantive impact of the deal will be minimal.

First, the competitiveness provisions are meaningless, merely reaffirming the European Union's commitment to strengthening the competitiveness of its single market. The agreement needed to include language on competitiveness as Cameron had listed this as one of four key areas of reform, but in practice enhancing competitiveness of the single market was a goal that member states and EU institutions shared in any case. For instance, in November 2014 the newly installed European Commission led by Jean-Claude Juncker made boosting EU competitiveness one of its key priorities.

YVES HERMAN / REUTERS

British Prime Minister David Cameron waves as he leaves a European Union leaders summit in Brussels February 20, 2016.

Economic governance sections aimed to protect British financial firms and to strengthen the firewall between EU countries that use the euro and those, like the United Kingdom, that do not. Negotiators agreed to prohibit the European Union from taking actions that unfairly discriminate against firms located in states that do not use the euro, affirm that EU financial regulators will not exercise authority over British financial institutions, and absolves London from participating in bailouts for nations that use the common currency. For the most part, however, these measures only reaffirm the status quo: the European Court has already banned preferential treatment for countries that use the euro, and the new deal still requires British financial regulators to apply the eurozone's financial rules. Likewise, the section on bailouts merely confirms what has already been in effect since the third Greek bailout in the summer of 2015, when EU leaders had agreed to exempt the United Kingdom and other non-Eurozone states from contributing to Eurozone bailouts.

The revised deal includes some sections that affirm state sovereignty. These too are largely symbolic. The United Kingdom won an explicit exemption from EU treaty language on the goal of "ever closer union," but this language never had any binding legal effect in the first place. The agreement also introduced a so-called "red card" system for national parliaments, which requires EU legislation to be amended or abandoned if more than 55 percent of national parliaments within the European Union object to it. The new red card system will likely prove meaningless, however. National governments, who are supposed to represent their national parliaments, are already key actors in the EU legislative process, and any proposal opposed by 55 percent of national parliaments would likely be blocked by national governments in any case.

Most importantly, the deal addressed immigration—the central issue driving support for Brexit across the United Kingdom. There is a widespread perception in the country, particularly among those supporting Brexit, that EU migrants see the country as a "honeypot nation" and are taking advantage of its benefits system. To address such concerns, Cameron had hoped to eliminate child benefits for EU citizens who work in the United Kingdom and have left their children in their home country. Eastern European EU members, led by Poland, rejected this demand, ultimately settling on a compromise that allowed the United Kingdom and other states to tie their payments to the standard of living where the child resides.

Cameron had also hoped to ban payment of "in-work" benefits, such as tax credits for low-wage workers, for newly arrived EU migrants working in the United Kingdom for the first four years. EU leaders rejected the outright ban he initially sought and agreed to a so-called "emergency brake" through which a state experiencing an inflow of workers of "exceptional magnitude" can restrict benefits temporarily, but only with the authorization of the European Council and only "to the extent necessary." Here too, Cameron's efforts have accomplished little: new provisions may limit the amount of government benefits given to migrant workers in the United Kingdom, but they will do little to affect the real underlying issue of concern to pro-Brexit campaigners— namely the total number of workers who enter the country every year.Numerous studies indicate that EU citizens come to the United Kingdom to obtain higher wages and better opportunities, rather thang to take advantage of social benefits.

WHAT'S REALLY AT STAKE?

Critics are right to argue that Cameron's deal for the United Kingdom changes little in practice. If anything, it simply reinforces the longstanding trend toward a "two-speed" Europe, in which some member economies seek more integration than others. The United Kingdom opted-out of the eurozone and the Schengen passport-free travel area a long time ago, and core eurozone countries pledged to move ahead with deeper integration in turn. Last week's deal affirms that split, but the details of the agreement will fade into the background as the Brexit debate focuses on how leaving the European Union would impact the United Kingdom's economy and national security.

Even under the most optimistic scenarios, three quarters of economists in a recent Financial Times poll agreed that the United Kingdom stands to gain very little from leaving the European Union. More than 40 percent of British exports go to the European single market. To maintain access to this market, the United Kingdom would have to agree to implement all EU directives and regulations, just as outsidersSwitzerland and Norway are forced to do today. In other words, the United Kingdom would lose all of its influence over EU legislation, but would still have to follow it. And even with a free trade arrangement with the European Union, new barriers to entry would be erected gradually, particularly in those areas (such as financial services) where the United Kingdom enjoys a comparative advantage and major trade surplus with other EU countries. Of course, London would remain Europe's leading financial center in the short and medium term, but without unfettered access to the single market, it could gradually lose some of its allure.

Outside the Union, the United Kingdom would have to renegotiate all its current free trade deals with the rest of the world, and would be dropped from the ongoing Transatlantic Trade and Investment Partnership negotiations with the United States. The United Kingdom is likely to get less attractive terms on its own than it would as a member of the European Union—the world's largest economic bloc. Foreign direct investment would suffer as investors turned their attention to countries such as Germany, Ireland, and the Netherlands that assure full access to the EU single market.

PHIL NOBLE / REUTERS

Badges with logos encouraging people to leave the EU are seen for sale on a stall at the UKIP party's spring conference, in Llandudno, Britain February 27, 2016.

Worst of all, restricting EU immigration would be very costly to the British economy: *Financial Times* columnist Martin Sandbu calculated that every Eastern European immigrant who arrived in the United Kingdom in the 2000s contributed on average almost $14,000 in fiscal benefits for the country over the decade (while each native citizen cost the country just under $21,000 over the same period). If a Brexit were to occur, EU workers in Britain could be thrown into a legal quagmire, with many deciding to return home. The legal status of roughly two million British citizens living in the rest of the European Union could also be called into question.

From a security point of view, it is hard to make the case that the United Kingdom will somehow be safer if it leaves the European Union. Many potential threats to national security such as Islamist terrorism, cyber security, and international crime networks are dealt with collaboratively at the EU level. As Europol director Robert Wainwright has said, outside the European Union, the United Kingdom would find it harder "to protect the citizens from terrorism and organized crime." Although an independent United Kingdom would remain a member of NATO and a permanent member of the UN Security Council, it would lose its leadership role in the European Union's fledgling foreign policy—an effort that has recently proved its effectiveness by imposing collective sanctions against Russia in reaction to its aggression in Ukraine. As Cameron pointed out during a debate in the House of Commons after the Brussels meeting, "the only person [he could] think of who would like [Britain] to leave the EU, is Vladimir Putin." Without British leadership, the European Union's common security and defense policy will falter, and history has shown that the United Kingdom cannot isolate itself from insecurity and conflict on the European continent for very long.

Lastly, some point to the current migration crisis and the unraveling of the Schengen passport-free zone as reasons the United Kingdom should leave the European Union. Indeed, the Schengen area is in shambles, and EU border security is deeply flawed. But as it stands, the United Kingdom already controls its own borders. It has chosen to stay out of the Schengen zone, and faces no requirement to join it in the future. And in terms of illegal immigration, a departure from the European Union will not forestall the desperate refugees residing in "the jungle" in Calais from trying to make the journey across the channel.

TIME TO DECIDE

The debate about Brexit remained on the back burner while Cameron negotiated with his EU counterparts over the past six months. Only now are many British voters beginning to pay attention to the debate, and Brexit opinion polls suggest a very close contest. Most analysts continue to believe that in the end, the British people will decide that they have too much to lose from Brexit and will choose to remain in the Union. But as the recent election of Labour leader Jeremy Corbyn demonstrates, anything can happen in contemporary British politics. The population is fed up with its political elites, and a referendum vote serves as a perfect opportunity to stick it to the governing class. As the European Union continues to suffer from multiple crises, the British people may well be in the mood for a fight. And this in turn might well result in a narrow vote to leave the union. And as both EU leaders and Cameron himself have made crystal clear after the summit, that decision will not be reversible.

Whatever the outcome, the referendum will be an expression of British sovereignty. The Brexit camp has argued that the European Union erodes their country's autonomy, and London Mayor Boris Johnson makes a valid point when he observes that the EU project has "morphed and grown in such a way as to be unrecognizable." Indeed, the scope of the European Union's powers has grown incredibly since the United Kingdom joined the European Economic Community back in 1973. Many British euroskeptics agree with Johnson that today's European Union is no longer the free trade club they thought they had signed up for under Prime Minister Edward Heath.

And yet, the very fact that the United Kingdom can hold a referendum on its EU membership exposes the fundamental flaw in the argument that British sovereignty has been compromised. If anything, the referendum should remind us that the European Union is and always has been a voluntary union. EU members must follow the union's rules and obey its courts, but they are free to quit at any time. Brexit would deal a huge blow to the European Union, and could even trigger exit referenda in other EU member states. But Brexit could also cause significant damage to the United Kingdom's own economic and security interests. Whatever the consequences, the British are free to choose their path and take their chances.

R. DANIEL KELEMEN is Professor of Political Science at Rutgers University and the editor of *Lessons From Europe? What Americans Can Learn From European Public Policies*. MATTHIAS MATTHIJS is Assistant Professor of International Political Economy at Johns Hopkins University's School of Advanced International Studies and the co-editor of *The Future of the Euro*.

Referendum Revenge

Putting a Safety Valve on Democracy

R. James Breiding

Emptying ballot boxes during elections for the Swiss Parliament in Bern, Switzerland, December 2015.

In the wake of last year's dramatic vote on the Greek bailout and ahead of the Brexit showdown, referendums are getting a bad rap. Last week, in an article titled "Let the people fail to decide," The Economist noted that such votes can "lead to incoherent policies," and thus "fewer would be better." Not to be undone, John Kay of the Financial Times warned against the tendency to "confuse democracy with populism," drawing from British statesman Edmund Burke's famous 1774 speech in which he argued "your representative owes you, not his industry only, but his judgment: and he betrays, instead of serving you, if he sacrifices it to your opinion."

Are they missing anything?

Whatever drawbacks referendums may have, they are the only true form of democracy. The United Kingdom, like most modern countries, is a nation in which power resides in representatives who are supposed to follow the preferences and will of their constituents but are removed from them. Switzerland is the closest to what Aristotle, Plato, and Socrates had in mind when democracy was conceived. The country has had 611 referendums since it was established in 1848, on issues ranging from abortion to asking taxpayers to pay for the children's national zoo.

No system is perfect. Referendums are disruptive and laborious, and they can be abused if issues qualify too easily. The yes-or-no nature of the decisions makes it easier for majorities to ride roughshod over minority interests. People also need to exercise sufficient care to form their judgement on the matter at hand, and then make the effort to vote.

Sometimes referendums make things messier. For instance, in 2014 Swiss voters approved by a slim majority a measure to limit immigration, in violation of the country's agreement with the European Union. The EU says the vote could jeopardize Switzerland's access to the European market, and it remains to be seen whether the treaties can be renegotiated. Voter turnout rates average about 42 percent in Switzerland, lower than for candidate elections, since voting on issues requires greater effort. However, turnout can be very high for hotly debated issues; for example, the turnout for the immigration initiative was 64 percent.

KEVIN COOMBS / REUTERS

A woman hands out leaflets campaigning to stay in Europe for the Brexit vote in London, Britain, May 2016.

There are, however, considerable advantages to having a dose of referendums every now and again. The ancient Greeks were wary of mob rule and felt that they were good opportunities to vent anger and act as circuit breakers to placate crowds and keep them from throwing rocks—as may occur at the forthcoming Republican National Convention in Cleveland. The debate and choice involved in a referendum also center on a particular issue rather than a personality or a political party. Just follow a few days of press coverage in the United States and the United Kingdom and compare the emphasis on personal attacks versus policy content.

Referendums also force voters to have skin in the game. It is easy to blame a politician for disappointing us, but who is to blame when we've made the choice ourselves? The debate over Brexit shows that people care, and caring is the foundation of any well functioning democracy.

Most importantly, referendums mitigate three of the most toxic features of republics. Elected officials have incentives to overpromise and under-deliver, so disappointment is practically pre-programmed. They are also encouraged to accelerate the benefits for "right now" and postpone the payment to "later," which punishes future generations. Third, lobbying is more cost-effective when a few politicians can be swayed to support a particular interest. Convincing large numbers of people requires greater transparency and more intense deliberation. As Jürgen Habermas, the famous German philosopher, argued, "the better the debate, the better the decision." His words may have even inspired the founders of The Economist when they penned their mantra: "to take part in a severe contest between intelligence which presses forward, and an unworthy, timid ignorance obstructing our progress."

ARND WIEGMANN / REUTERS

A man walks past a poster of the Swiss People's Party demanding 'Stop - Yes to ban of minarets' at the central station in Zurich ahead of a refendum in October 2009.

Switzerland, that bastion of popular votes, has been ranked by the World Economic Forum as the most economically competitive country in the world for seven years running. It has among the lowest rates of unemployment, crime, public deficits, and CO2 emissions. It has among the highest per capita incomes, confidence levels in its government, and funding of its pension schemes. The Economist even ranked it last year as the country in which one would most wish to be born—without seeming to fully understand what has made it this way. The Swiss have achieved this in good part by repeatedly voting in referendums for no shorter work weeks, enforcing a debt moratorium on parliament, passing laws to encourage the use of renewable energy, and even voting to increase taxes that were necessary to become more fiscally sound.

Compare this to the record of countries such as the United Kingdom and others. The deficiencies such an exercise would reveal may explain why the people of the United Kingdom, United States, and elsewhere are increasingly frustrated with their political systems that are more dependent on representatives. Fewer than three in ten Americans trust their federal government (slightly higher than the level of trust in a used car salesman), down precipitously from nearly eight in ten one generation ago, according to Pew Research Center. The United Kingdom has experienced a more moderate, yet similar, decline.

If nations were able to attract candidates of Edmund Burke's quality and stature, then there might not be a need for referendums. But this seems unrealistic. The Swiss model turns the equation on its head, based on the premise that there are too few

Edmund Burkes alive and that we should not rely on them anyway. The robustness of a system is measured by how much abuse it can withstand. It is far better to engineer a system to ensure that politicians, even the inferior ones, manage to serve their constituents' interests.

Referendums can be decisive in this respect. Yet The Economist criticized referendums because "they tend to make politicians look as if they do not know what they are doing."

Precisely. The Swiss can call referendums to challenge and reverse legislation passed by parliament. Such votes have succeeded only two percent of the time, according to Laurent Bernard from the Institute of Political Science at the University of Zurich. (Around six percent of the laws passed by parliament have been challenged by referendum so far, with 178 referendums.) But the very possibility of repudiation, and the embarrassment that ensues, may be the reason challenges are so rare and may be the most effective control to ensure that what parliament does is what the people want.

Switzerland is not alone. Sweden voted against using the euro in 2003; Chile voted for free schooling for everyone in 2011; New Zealand opposed a partial privatization of public-owned companies in 2013; Uruguay decided not to lower the age of criminal responsibility to 16 years in 2014; Ireland refused to abolish its Senate in 2013; and Bulgaria accepted the construction of a nuclear plant in 2013.

Such successes show that the people as a whole can be a more reliable source of wisdom and positive outcomes than any group of politicians. At a time when people are increasingly disappointed with their political systems, it is worth reflecting on what has gone wrong and experiment with ways to fix it. In this respect, republics may find that more democracy is better than less.

R. JAMES BREIDING is the author of *Swiss Made—The Untold Story Behind Switzerland's Success* and Managing Director of Naissance Capital Ltd., a Switzerland-based investment firm.

The Conservative Case Against Brexit

Euroskepticism's Biggest Fallacy

Dalibor Rohac

Campaigners hold placards as British Prime Minister David Cameron delivers a speech at a 'Stronger In' campaign event in Witney, Oxfordshire, Britain, 14 May 2016.

It is now up to British voters to decide whether the United Kingdom should leave the European Union—not to foreign leaders, including U.S. President Barack Obama and IMF head Christine Lagarde, who have offered their advice on what the right choice might be. The voters, however, would do well not to automatically dismiss what Obama and Lagarde have said. Rather, they should reflect on their substantive merits.

The truth is that the case for "Brexit" does not hold water. Although there is much to criticize about the EU, its existence is an important achievement, which would be put in peril by the United Kingdom's departure from the bloc. Conservatives, classical liberals, and advocates of free markets should be particularly wary of becoming cheerleaders for the EU's demise. Instead, they ought to be at the forefront of efforts to reform and improve the bloc.

Free-marketeers and small-c conservatives might see Euroskepticism as a natural extension of free-market convictions. For fervent believers in the strength of competition, including between different currencies and regulatory and tax systems, European integration might look like a misguided attempt at integrating markets via the unnecessary centralization of political decision-making. And so it seems logical for the president of the Czech Republic, Václav Klaus, to compare the EU to the former Soviet Union, and for free-market think tanks to criticize the EU's populist overregulation, common currency, and common agricultural policy, among other things.

But Euroskepticism is not an inevitable corollary of free-market conservative thought—something that the iconic voices of the free-market movement well understood. Friedrich von Hayek wanted a European federation. He called "the abrogation of national sovereignties" that it would entail a "logical consummation of the liberal [i.e. free-market] programme." Hayek, who later received the Nobel Prize for Economics, recognized that the efforts to liberalize trade in the nineteenth century had ultimately failed because European countries lacked a joint system of governance that would keep domestic protectionism and nationalism at bay.

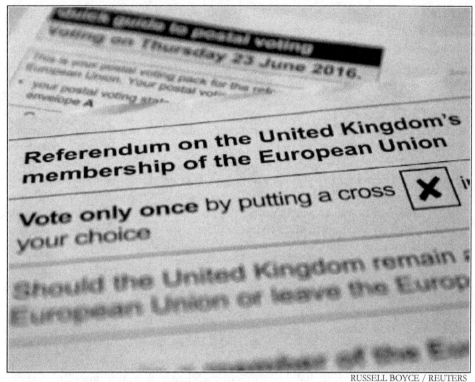

Illustration picture of postal ballot papers June 1, 2016 ahead of the June 23 BREXIT referendum when voters will decide whether Britain will remain in the European Union.

Hayek's thinking on international federalism developed alongside that of Wilhelm Röpke, a German free-market economist who argued that Europe's postwar reconstruction should involve a scaling up of the Swiss model of governance to the international realm, since that would allow the creation of a system of governance that would be simultaneously decentralized and allow for the joint provision of fundamental, pan-European public goods—especially economic openness and security.

Even Hayek's mentor, Ludwig von Mises, who was generally seen as a much more radical free-marketeer than his protegé, wrote in 1944 that for Western European countries, "the alternative to incorporation into a new democratic supernational system is not unrestricted sovereignty but ultimate subjugation by the totalitarian powers." And, when British Prime Minister Margaret Thatcher campaigned for the United Kingdom's membership in the European Economic Community in 1975, she recognized that "almost every major nation has been obliged...to pool significant areas of sovereignty so as to create more effective political units."

Today's world is very different from that of the 1940s or the 1970s. But that does not make the European project irrelevant. Quite the contrary. Even the seemingly economic components of European integration, such as the single market, require a significant pooling of political sovereignty, a bureaucracy, and courts to enforce the rules. In part, this is because a single market goes far beyond the question of the tariffs that, until 1968, separated markets in the countries of the European Economic Area. It has sought to curb regulatory protectionism and other, more subtle barriers to trade, including distortionary state aid spending directed at national champions.

The single market did not arise overnight. It took decades of political and legislative effort, most notably in the form of the Single European Act, spearheaded by Thatcher and Conservative politician and eventual European Commissioner Arthur Cockfield, to reach the degree of economic openness existing in the EU today. The single market is perhaps the most striking example of what the EU does best—namely, that it serves as a commitment device.

When Euroskeptics complain of the constraints that European integration imposes on national sovereignty, they are thus missing the point. European treaties, the entire body of EU law, and the decision-making authorities disentangled from national politics exist for a good reason—to allow politicians in member states to get around the problem of credible commitment, which is pervasive in democracies, and which involves the omnipresent temptation of policymakers to renege on their promises.

The United Kingdom benefits greatly from the "financial passport" that allows its banks and other financial businesses to operate anywhere in the EU.

To see how, look to Eastern European reformers in places such as Slovakia or Poland who used the prospect of EU accession as a sweetener for domestic reforms that would have otherwise been unpalatable. For countries such as France or Italy, EU policy is often the only thing that keeps their leaders from returning to their countries' historic traditions of providing state aid to national champions. It was, after all, the European Commission that forced Italy to dismantle its state-owned steel industry in the 1990s and pushed France toward the opening of its electricity market in 1999. Without the United Kingdom's voice at the table, the EU would inevitably become a much weaker force for economic liberalization, and some of prior achievements could even be reversed.

Euroskeptics have a point when they say that there is a flipside to the single market—namely, the existence of a large and burdensome system of regulation at the European level. It would be much better, they argue, if member states simply recognized each other's regulations and technical standards without imposing a one-size-fits-all solution on everyone. But unconditional mutual recognition is not realistic—largely because governments are unable to commit credibly to such a policy. Hence, although common EU directives certainly impose a burden on the European economy, that burden needs to be compared against the burden of 28 different and potentially incompatible regulatory systems, hindering free movement of goods, services, capital, and people.

The United Kingdom, with its sizeable sector of financial services, benefits greatly from the "financial passport" that allows its banks and other financial businesses to operate anywhere in the EU. The City of London is also home to the European Banking Authority, an EU-wide financial regulator, over which the United Kingdom has had a significant influence. A departure from the EU could jeopardize these arrangements and raise doubts about the future of the city as the world's financial capital.

A car sticker with a logo encouraging people to leave the EU is seen on a car, in Llandudno, Wales, February 27, 2016.

The complaint about EU regulation is just one example of the nirvana fallacy of Euroskepticism. No one would deny that the European Union is a highly flawed organization. However, it makes no sense to compare it to impossible alternatives. The relevant counterfactual to today's European Union is the Europe of protectionist, nationalist states that was long the baseline of the continent's history.

Even the late nineteenth century, sometimes called the First Age of Globalization, was the period of German Chancellor Otto von Bismarck's "iron and rye" tariff, France's Méline tariff, and a continent-wide drift toward protectionism. In 1913, tariffs on manufactured goods averaged 18 percent in Austria-Hungary, 13 percent in Germany, 20 percent in France, 41 percent in Spain, and a staggering 84 percent in Russia. At that time, the United Kingdom appeared a free-trading nation in comparison, with no tariffs on manufactured goods and an average applied tariff of around 5 percent on all imports. Yet, throughout much of the nineteenth century, until the late 1870s, the UK was highly protectionist, with average tariffs exceeding those in France.

With the advent of World War I, followed by the Great Depression and then by the bloodiest conflict in human history, international trade essentially collapsed, greatly exacerbating the human misery that characterized the first half of the twentieth century. By that token, the past 70 years of European history, during which Europe has become more economically open, democratic, and peaceful than ever before, are a complete historical anomaly. Whether one believes that the EU deserves any credit for this outcome, one should think twice before trying to tinker with the system of international political architecture existing in Europe.

The United Kingdom's leadership has been essential for the existence and success of this system, including the single market but also in focusing Europe's attention to the threats facing the continent, such as the rise of a revisionist Russia. And although the United Kingdom can prosper even outside of the EU, Brexit would inevitably set in motion centrifugal dynamics on the continent, empowering nationalists in countries that have no chance of being successful outside of the EU. Just a few weeks ago, inspired by the upcoming British referendum, 92 out of 200 members of the Czech Parliament voted for the motion—narrowly defeated—to organize a referendum about the departure of the Czech Republic from the EU.

At the present time, Europe is coming under an unprecedented amount of stress. From the economic woes of the eurozone, through the political tensions brought about by the refugee crisis, to Russian President Vladimir Putin's use of propaganda and energy ties to undermine liberal democracy in Central and Eastern Europe, the continent is at a greater risk of descending into chaos than at any point in its postwar history. That is the real danger facing Europeans today, not the threat of a Pan-European authoritarian superstate.

It is imperative that the proponents of free markets, both classical liberal and conservative, double down on their defense of the international political order in Europe, which has coincided with the continent's current period of peace, democracy, and prosperity.

DALIBOR ROHAC is a Research Fellow at the American Enterprise Institute and the author of *Towards an Imperfect Union: A Conservative Case for the EU*.

PLEASE LEAVE

WHY BREXIT WOULD BENEFIT EUROPE

CAMILLE PECASTAING

People waving British flags wait for Britain's Prince William and his wife Catherine, Duchess of Cambridge, to appear at the balcony of Buckingham Palace after their wedding in London, April 2011.

If Europe were a democracy, all of its citizens would have had a say in whether the United Kingdom leaves or remains in the European Union. After all, it is not the just the fate of the British that Brexit would affect, but also the quality and longevity of the entire European project. The EU, as it turns 65, is showing grave sclerosis, and voices—nationalist, populist, and sometimes xenophobic—are calling for its dissolution. The moment has thus come, if it has not already passed, to prune the dead wood of the tree to save the trunk.

The European Union's original mission was more political than economic, as were its greatest successes. The union was designed to put an end to perpetual conflict between France and Germany. It succeeded, ending a millennium of intra-European wars in the process. The union also brilliantly helped Eastern European countries quickly transition from decades of Russian tutelage following the disintegration of the Soviet Union. In parallel to the political project, over the decades, Europeans created an integrated economic space, culminating in theadoption of a single currency at the turn of the millennium.

The problem is that, over time, the economic dimension of the European project has overtaken its political and cultural aspects. Losing sight of all that Europe could be, the poorest regions and members came to see the union as a giant ATM. The richest believed it to be a money pit for their taxes. The United Kingdom, more than anyone else, has been aware of those tensions and has exploited them since the days of Margaret Thatcher. By doing so, it has reinforced public perceptions that membership in the union is a zero-sum game, especially when money is tight.

Yves Herman / REUTERS
British Prime Minister David Cameron with French President Francois Hollande, German Chancellor Angela Merkel, Italian Prime Minister Matteo Renzi, and Donald Tusk, then prime minister of Poland, at a meeting of European leaders on the Ukraine crisis in Brussels, March 2014.

The United Kingdom's position in Europe was always uncomfortable. During the 1960s, its accession to the common market was repeatedly vetoed by French President Charles de Gaulle, who denounced London as a Trojan horse for Washington's interference. In reality, de Gaulle feared that British membership would dilute Paris' influence. The Europe he envisioned was built around a Franco-German axis dominated by France, if only because of all the restrictions imposed on Germany after WWII. But with de Gaulle out of power, membership came for the United

Kingdom in 1973, and with it came the triangular relationship that the French and Germans finally accepted with relief. Germany dreaded France's excessive ambitions, including breaking away from NATO's unified command and embarking on grandiose industrial projects—one of which, the Airbus Group, owes its ultimate success to German realism. As for France, the recession of 1973 marked the beginning of continuous economic decline in relation to Germany, which also became demographically dominant when its eastern and western halves reunified in 1990. When it needed to, Paris could ally with London to stand up to Bonn—later Berlin—as it did recently in the war in Libya.

Throughout, the United Kingdom remained a marginal partner, but the price it exacted for its arbitrage was exorbitant, including exemptions from membership rules—the United Kingdom stayed out of Schengen, out of the euro—and financial concessions to boot—the infamous British rebate on dues, negotiated by Margaret Thatcher, that has applied every year since 1985. In the process, London's approach to Europe scuttled any momentum toward federalism, turning a project that aspired to strong political union into nothing more than an ever-enlarging free market.

Brexit could be the best thing for Europe since the fall of the Berlin Wall.

The United Kingdom was not alone in exploiting the situation, and this is where the case for Brexit echoes last year's case for Grexit. Greece, an underdeveloped country that joined the EU in 1981, has used the union foremost as a source of foreign aid and, when the euro was adopted, of almost free loans guaranteed by the union's richer members. It was a flagrant abuse of the spirit of the union, but Greece was economically marginal. Its profligacy went unremarked until the global economic meltdown that began in 2007.

Even then, ever opposed to Grexit, the union decided to throw good money after bad rather than set a precedent for departure from the eurozone. Eurocrats have met Brexit with the same anxiety, handing British Prime Minister David Cameron yet more special treatment for the United Kingdom—only in Britain would recent EU migrants be denied access to welfare and other benefits—and put yet more nails in the federalist coffin. The hope was that those concessions, coupled with a massive campaign of economic fearmongering, into which the IMF and even U.S. President Barack Obama were drafted, would sway British voters to stay in the union.

Whether those efforts have paid off will become apparent on June 23, when voters across the United Kingdom go to the polls. The British, who have stymied Europe for decades, now have a chance to set it free. If anything, the Greek crisis has shown that greater federalism is the only way forward for Europe, because monetary decisions related to the euro should be backed up by fiscal policies, which should be approved by union-wide democratic consultation. In some respects, the EU looks a lot like the United States, with some areas of productive brilliance—Silicon Valley, which is akin to Germany's Mittelstand—subsidizing deadbeats elsewhere. But the United States, for all its local particularism, is still a country with a nation that accepts that taxes from California will pay for public schools in Mississippi. It is that redistributive logic that makes a commonwealth and that, in Europe, the Greeks have abused and the British have denied. And this is why Europe would be better off without them.

PHIL NOBLE / REUTERS

A banner encouraging people to support a local Brexit campaign hangs on the side of a building in the English town of Altrincham, May 2016.

Mississippi may never become another Silicon Valley, but because the United States is one country, there is no fundamental reason why it should not. Europe is different, because claims of national distinctiveness—traditionally, the French never work on Sundays—thwart the dissemination of efficiency-related best practices—like opening stores on Sundays. Germans may not be too keen on dominical work either, but there is no question that Germany's overall socioeconomic model is more efficient than France's. And yet, a sovereign French government has struggled for decades to push forward reforms that would increase competitiveness. A federation, especially one dominated by efficient Germany yet structurally democratic, would find it easier to disseminate and enforce best practices. But such a project requires more commitment than Athens and London are willing to make.

Quite apart from questions of what the United Kingdom will gain from leaving the EU, it is certain that the shock of its departure will deliver much-needed (if bitter) medicine to a gravely ill patient. All in all, the benefit that is an opportunity of finally fulfilling the European dream of political union would far exceed the short-term disadvantages of a British secession. The economic shock from Brexit is bound to be moderate in comparison to the financial crises of the last decades, from which a resilient global economy recovered. And whatever validation Brexit gives to the many voices that push nationalist priorities over continental ones, British secession would also free federal-minded leaders to present voters with a more ambitious, more coherent, and more inspirational project. In short, Brexit could be the best thing for Europe since the fall of the Berlin Wall.

CAMILLE PECASTAING is Senior Associate Professor of Middle East Studies at Johns Hopkins University's School of Advanced International Studies.

June 22, 2016

Leveraging Leave

The Pragmatic Case for Brexit

Douglas Murray

NEIL HALL / REUTERS

After a pro-EU public event in London, June 2016.

Thursday is referendum day in the United Kingdom, and politicians and pundits from all sides of the debate are trying to cram in their last words. Those who believe that the country should opt to remain in the EU are reiterating all their well-worn economic arguments; those in favor of leaving are once again focusing on sovereignty and border control. Both are portraying themselves as making the positive case in a season of political negativity.

Those foundations are the renegotiation of the United Kingdom's relationship with the EU that British Prime Minister David Cameronundertook in Brussels earlier this year. He went to the bargaining table with five key demands. At the time, polls suggested that around two-thirds of British adults would vote to remain in the EU if Cameron won on those points (which included an attempted exemption from the commitment to an "ever-closer union"). Only 26 percent were willing to leave regardless.

DAN KITWOOD / POOL / REUTERS

British Prime Minister David Cameron at a meeting with European Council President Donald Tusk and European Commission President Jean Claude Juncker during a European Union leaders summit in Brussels, February 2016.

It was thus vital for the prime minister and his supporters to insist that he came out of the fray with what he had said he would. But even that is much debated. And one nugget that the "Remain" camp is intent to overlook is not only the unambitious nature of the original renegotiation but also the fact that the resulting agreement has still not been ratified by the other member states. Even if the British public ticks "Remain" on Thursday, in other words, there is still no certainty that the United Kingdom's European partners would hold up their end of the deal.

Perhaps it is inevitable that, in a campaign based on a black- and-white choice, both sides should play down any gray areas. After all, that is how Cameron planned it. By making the vote come down to either approving his new deal or leaving the EU entirely, the prime minister obviously hoped to clarify, if not simplify, the issue. He was banking on the hope that many of those who are highly critical of the EU might nevertheless balk at the idea of leaving it entirely. Yet in recent weeks, a number of polls have consistently shown "Leave" ahead of "Remain," and Downing Street has gone into a partial panic. Now, in the hours before the vote, the "Remain" campaign has harped on about there being no going back from a vote to get out.

For the United Kingdom and Europe, the only question is which variety of unpredictability we will choose.

Yet plenty of Brussels-watchers are dubious. The EU has never been good at giving up power, and it has excelled at ignoring electorates. Readers will recall the moment in 2005 when the Dutch and French publics were invited to vote to ratify a new EU constitution that involved further integration. Both electorates declined the offer, only for the EU to push on. Likewise, in Ireland, the EU fell back on its habit of asking the public to vote and then asking them to vote again (or simply ignoring the result) when the electorate came up with the wrong answer.

From the very outset of the Brexit debate, there were those—including former London Mayor Boris Johnson, who favors leaving—who suggested that a "Leave" vote might not, in fact, be a vote to fully leave, but a signal to Brussels that the United Kingdom demands a deeper renegotiation that results in more substantial opt-outs and other special treatment. This line of thinking was swiftly brushed aside, both by the prime minister, who needed the vote to look final, and by the "Leave" campaign, which couldn't look as though it wanted out but only sort of.

But after Thursday, all such gray areas may well be explored. Although a significant victory for "Remain" (a win by a ten percent margin or more) might well satisfy the country that the issue had gone away, it might also satisfy its EU partners that further British obstreperousness is both unwarranted and insincere. If 60 percent of the voting public says that it wishes to remain in the EU, then future British governments of any political stripe will hardly be able to keep playing their traditional card, which they have used to great effect, of threatening fellow Europeans with a UK exit. After all, should Cameron or any other future prime minister warn of deep euroskepticism among the British public, Brussels would understandably just point to the recent referendum. And so whatever British leverage does exist will be lost.

David Cameron and George Osborne in Blackpool, England, October 2007.

Should the vote be close (a 52 percent win for "Remain," for instance), then the British people could still plausibly feel that the issue of the EU had not gone away and the European Commission—sensing the long-term repercussions—might be more willing to rein in its expansionist tendencies. The eurocrats may have ignored the Dutch, French, and Irish electorates in the past (not to mention the Greeks) but it is possible that a knife-edge result would give future British negotiators a useful deterrent.

The United Kingdom could use its new leverage to push for any number of reforms, from changes to EU fishing and agricultural policy all the way to migrant quotas, the most toxic issues over which the EU is currently losing its public support. (By contrast, a United Kingdom that had voted 60-40 in favor of "Remain" would find it exceptionally difficult to avoid whatever migration obligations the commission forces on it.) The same applies to a shared financial obligation when, as expected, Greece defaults on its next round of debt repayments next month. A union in which the United Kingdom overwhelmingly votes to remain is not a Europe in which the United Kingdom can quite so readily pick and choose. The country will have obligations that it will—quite rightly—have to fulfill.

All these options have been, to some extent, raised in the public debate. The one that has been utterly quashed is what would happen if British voters opt to leave. Contrary to the prime minister's insistence that "Leave" means go, it is perfectly imaginable that after such a vote, the EU would go into panic mode. It could very well step in with an offer of a meaningful renegotiation. A new deal's makeup would depend both on what other EU members offer and also on who is in Downing Street this time next week. For if the country votes "Leave," even Cameron's closest allies admit, he will have his own exit to make. His chancellor and right-hand man, George Osborne, will almost certainly leave office, too. The whole country—and indeed continent—will be in the realm of the unknowable. Perhaps it was always so. But for the United Kingdom and Europe, the only question is which variety of unpredictability we will choose.

DOUGLAS MURRAY is Associate Director of The Henry Jackson Society.

© Foreign Affairs

The New Divided Kingdom

A Brexit Post-Mortem

JOHN MCCORMICK

A taxi driver holds a Union flag, London, United Kingdom, June 24, 2016.

On June 24, the world awoke to find itself facing the inconceivable: the United Kingdom had voted—52 to 48 percent—to leave the European Union, defying predictions and what some considered all rationality.

It may be difficult to recall that only four years ago the EU had received the Nobel Prize for, as the committee put it, contributing six decades "of peace and reconciliation, democracy, and human rights in Europe." And yet one single but mighty vote has potentially set in motion the unraveling of the European project.

The immediate fallout included the resignation of the man who called for the referendum, Prime Minister David Cameron, as well as turmoil in international markets, disbelief among other EU and world leaders, and disquiet in Washington. Domestically, the divisions that led to Brexit have only worsened. Cameron decided to hold the referendum in large part to quell infighting within the Conservative Party and to stem growing support for the nationalist United Kingdom Independence Party. Instead, the in-out campaign unleashed ugly emotions and even violence, culminating in the murder of pro-EU Member of Parliament Jo Cox by a man with possible right-wing links.

These sentiments pitted "leavers" against "remainers," old versus young; widened the cleavages in the major political parties; and fueled clashes among members of communities and even families. It has also embittered Scotland, Northern Ireland, and London, which all clearly favored "remain." Scotland's First Minister Nicola Sturgeon decried the outcome as "democratically unacceptable" and has now promised another vote for Scottish independence. Unlike the referendum in 2014, this one may very well lead to secession now that the region's EU membership is at stake.

The rest of Europe remains just as divided. The concern for Brussels is that other countries similarly torn over EU membership will be emboldened to hold their own national referendums. Marine Le Pen, the leader of France's right-wing National Front party, called Brexit a "victory" and tweeted that France needs a similar vote—the term "Frexit" is already being thrown around. And in that spirit, Geert Wilders, leader of the Dutch, anti-immigrant Party for Freedom, mentioned a "Nexit." Other far-right parties across Europe are echoing these calls. This disunion comes at a time when Europe is still struggling to recover from the eurozone crisis and resolve difficulties over the migrants pouring in from Syria.

To counter this, European Commission President Jean-Claude Juncker has demanded that the United Kingdom begin the exiting process immediately, perhaps intending to set an example of what will happen to any other country that decides to leave. The rules allow the United Kingdom two years of negotiation, but if no deal is agreed upon, it will have to return to its pre-1973 status. That was the year the United Kingdom joined what was then the European Economic Community, which was not much more than a single marketplace. Already, François Villeroy de Galhau, governor of the Bank of France and a member of the European Central Bank's Governing Council, has threatened to take back the United Kingdom's passporting rights, which allow international financial services to access the EU market while operating in the United Kingdom. But Matthew Elliott, chief executive of the Vote Leave campaign, scoffed at the idea, countering that any leave agreement would involve keeping those rights. He pointed to Norway, which has no voting rights in the EU but still has access to the single market and the privilege of passporting.

The EU is now sailing through uncharted waters, so it is unclear how exactly the negotiations to leave will unfold. There are even questions about whether the exit will happen, either wholly or in part. The referendum was advisory, and so the formal exit cannot happen without legislation from the British Parliament. Also, a petition to hold a second referendum has attracted more than one million signatures. There is further speculation that Scotland may not leave after all, and it is clear that many British voters are experiencing buyer's remorse; many have said they intended only to send a signal of protest, not to actually leave the bloc. The United Kingdom is clearly about to enter a messy and uncertain period. What impact this will have on the enthusiasm for exit movements in other EU countries will depend on the outcome of the next few months or even years.

To be sure, the EU was not perfect in the way it was structured or in the policies it pursued. Indeed, part of the motivation behind the British referendum was to allow voters to offer input on how to reform the United Kingdom's relationship with the EU. But the outcome has gone much further than Cameron or even many British Euroskeptics had wanted. Seen in this way, Brexit is a rude wake-up call to the governments of the other 27 member states and to the leaders of the major EU institutions. There are two potential silver linings to this dark cloud. First, it is possible, if difficult to imagine amid the current turmoil, that the EU could heed the call for reform and emerge from the Brexit debacle leaner, more efficient, and more closely attuned to what the European people want. Second, it could turn out that the costs of the referendum and of Brexit are so great for the United Kingdom—in political, economic, and social terms—that they will be enough to make other EU member states think twice about holding their own votes. The United Kingdom is a pioneer in this regard, and its experience may end up as a salutary warning for others.

JOHN MCCORMICK is Jean Monnet Professor of European Union Politics at Indiana University.

© Foreign Affairs

LONDON FALLING

LIFE AFTER BREXIT

R. DANIEL KELEMEN

In a historic act of self-harm, the British electorate has chosen to leave the European Union. Brexit—as it is called—will do severe damage to the United Kingdom's economy and its strategic interests. Brexit will also deal a heavy blow to the project of European integration. The EU will survive, but it will never be the same. Leaders of far-right parties across Europe cheered the referendum result, as did Donald Trump. Meanwhile, the United Kingdom's allies shuddered, and financial markets in the country and across the world plummeted.

With negotiations beginning over the terms of the United Kingdom's departure, much is uncertain. But one thing is clear already: the Leave campaign's claim that the

EU had robbed the United Kingdom of its sovereignty was false. If nothing else, the vote shows that the country was sovereign all along and that it was free to make disastrous decisions.

A TOXIC CAMPAIGN

The Leave victory marks the culmination of a poisonous debate. Although the Remain campaign was responsible for some distortions of its own—such as claiming that Brexit would make British households 4,300 pounds (over $5,000) worse off per year—the Leave campaign was premised on lies and empty promises. Proponents claimed that EU immigrants were to blame for the strains on Britain's public services, when in fact they made net contributions to the Exchequer, to the tune of 20 billion pounds (over $27 billion) between 2000 and 2011. Leave stoked xenophobia, suggesting that the EU was opening the United Kingdom to a flood of refugees and would soon allow millions of Turks to immigrate to Britain. Neither was true. In fact, London had complete control over how many refugees the United Kingdom accepted. Turkey is not "set to join the EU" as the Leave campaign claimed, and in any case, Britain had a veto over Turkish membership.

ANDREA COMAS / REUTERS

Electronic boards are seen at the Madrid stock exchange which plummeted after Britain voted to leave the European Union in the EU BREXIT referendum, in Madrid, Spain, June 24, 2016.

Leave leaders also appealed to "Little England's" worst nationalist instincts—repeatedly comparing the EU with Nazi Germany. The campaign's only real parallel with Nazism was UKIP leader Nigel Farage's "Breaking Point" poster, which closely resembled Nazi propaganda picturing a column of refugees.

Of course, the Remain campaign was lackluster. Although Prime Minister David Cameron spoke passionately for continued British membership in the EU, he and his Conservative pro-Remain colleagues lacked credibility after years of scoring cheap points by bashing Brussels. Labour leader Jeremy Corbyn, a long-time eurosceptic, damned the union with faint praise when he declared that he was "seven out of ten" for Remain. Polling in the run-up to the vote revealed that nearly half of Labour supporters were uncertain of their party's position on the referendum.

STUFF EU!

The Remain side lost despite enjoying the backing of labor unions, business leaders, universities, doctors, the governments of all of the United Kingdom's allies, celebrities ranging from David Beckham to J.K. Rowling, and the leadership of every party aside from UKIP. The Bank of England, the IMF, and an overwhelming majority of economists warned that Brexit would severely damage investment, growth, and jobs in Britain. A majority of voters just didn't care. Brexiteer Michael Gove was on to something when he said, "I think people in this country have had enough of experts."

To be sure, the Leave side was fueled by a populist backlash against elites. But the campaign itself was led by consummate members of the Tory party elite such as Etonian former London Mayor Boris Johnson and Lord Chancellor Gove. Also, the anti-establishment mood didn't seem to guide young voters: large majorities of those under 50 years old voted to stay, while it was those over 50 who pushed the United Kingdom out. Many frustrated young voters will feel that the old—nostalgic for a bygone Britain—have robbed them of a European future.

More than anything, though, the Leave vote was a vote against immigration. The closing days of the campaign revealed more starkly than ever just how central opposition to immigration was to the Leave campaign. Initial polling showed that nearly three-quarters of voters who saw immigration as the most important issue facing Britain favored Brexit, whereas strong majorities of those who saw economic issues as the main concern supported Remain.

The day after the vote, Britons—those who got any sleep—awoke to the sight of Cameron announcing that he will step down as prime minister in time for the Conservative Party conference in October. Although Cameron originally promised to stay on regardless of the result, that position was untenable after he led the losing Remain campaign. Whether or not Boris Johnson replaces Cameron, it is clear that the new leadership will come from the Brexiteer wing of the Conservative Party. And so, Cameron lost the gamble of his life. Having called for a referendum in hopes of staving off UKIP and containing the anti-EU wing of his own party, he will end up handing them control. The Labour Party is in turmoil as well, with Corbyn facing a leadership challenge from his backbenches.

A British flag which was washed away by heavy rains the day before lies on the street in London, Britain, June 24, 2016 after Britain voted to leave the European Union in the EU BREXIT referendum.

But divisions within the Conservatives and Labour are the least of the United Kingdom's worries now. With the pound plummeting to its lowest value in decades, stock markets around the world tumbling, and Standard & Poor's planning to strip the United Kingdom of its AAA status, the short-term economic consequences of Brexit are already apparent. The long-term economic and political consequences, although more uncertain, are potentially far more troubling.

Voters also awoke to a disunited Kingdom: the referendum map revealed a sharply divided nation, with Scotland, Northern Ireland, and London voting overwhelmingly for Remain, whereas most of the rest of England went for Leave. Scottish leaders have already declared that they should not be dragged out of the EU against their will by English voters and have called for a second referendum on Scottish independence. In Northern Ireland, too, some Sinn Fein leaders have called for a vote on leaving the United Kingdom to enter a union with the Republic of Ireland.

And as they begin to feel the economic pain of Brexit and contemplate the potential disintegration of the United Kingdom, it may also begin to dawn on Brexit supporters that the Leave campaign sold them a false bill of goods. Even before breakfast the morning after the vote, Farage declared that it had been "a mistake" to claim that the 350 million pounds a week (a widely discredited figure) that the United Kingdom would supposedly save by not paying into the EU budget would be directed to the National Heath Service. Brexit campaigner and Member of the European Parliament Daniel Hannan also clarified for voters that Brexit would not mean an end to EU immigration into Britain; instead, the government would now have control over who comes in and migrants would no longer enjoy the rights of EU citizens. Ultimately, Leave voters who were venting anger over economic insecurity, declining living standards, and recent cuts to public services will discover that structural changes in the economy and Conservative government policies—not the EU or migrants—were at the root of these problems.

IN A BIND?

Legally speaking, the referendum result is not binding. But politically, it would be practically impossible for the new leadership that replaces Cameron to ignore the result. In other words, the United Kingdom will soon set about the process of leaving the EU.

The EU treaties set out clear procedures in Article 50 through which member states may leave. According to the process, the United Kingdom must notify the European Council of its intention to leave the Union, which would then instigate a process of negotiation lasting up to two years—or longer, if all member states agree—to determine the terms of withdrawal. Cameron promised to launch Article 50 immediately after the referendum, but in announcing his resignation, he declared that Article 50 should only be invoked by his successor in the autumn. Some Brexit campaigners have hoped to avoid the procedure altogether (and with it avoid the proviso that the European Parliament must endorse any deal) and to negotiate informally with the European Union. But EU leaders have already stated their position emphatically: the United Kingdom must follow the Article 50 procedure, and start doing so as soon as possible.

No one can say for certain what the outcome of the negotiations will be. The Leave campaign was notoriously vague on the issue, but there are a few main options—each problematic in its own way. First, if the United Kingdom wants to retain full access to the EU's single market, it could follow the so-called Norwegian option and opt into the European Economic Area (EEA), which is an existing arrangement linking some neighboring countries to the EU's single market. Otherwise, the United Kingdom could follow the similar Swiss option, through which it would create a bilateral deal with the EU similar to the EEA arrangement.

But in these models, in exchange for access to the single market, the United Kingdom would have to allow free movement of labor, pay into the EU budget, and follow the EU's accumulated body of regulations—all things the Leave campaign promised would end with Brexit. In short, the United Kingdom would still be subject to single-market rules, but lose any role in shaping them. If, instead, the United Kingdom chooses to leave the single market entirely, it could trade with the EU like any other country that is a member of the WTO (the so-called WTO option). But in this case, British firms would face tariffs as well as substantial non-tariff barriers to trade. Given that 44 percent of British exports go the European Union's single market, such an outcome would be damaging indeed.

In negotiating with the United Kingdom, the EU will face contradictory pressures. On the one hand, given the size and importance of the British economy, the EU will want to maintain a vibrant trading relationship. A deep recession in an economically isolated Britain would hurt continental Europe as well. On the other hand, the EU needs to drive a hard bargain with Britain to discourage any other member states from considering withdrawal. The EU must send a strong signal that leaving has costly consequences and demonstrate, as Jean-Claude Juncker put it on the eve of the referendum, that "out is out."

AFTER BREXIT

In a European Union beset by problems—economic and monetary breakdown, refugees, and democratic backsliding in the east—Brexit is the greatest of them all. Support for the EU is at an all-time low, and the Leave victory has been cheered by far-right leaders, from France's Marine Le Pen to the Netherlands' Geert Wilders, who have called for referenda of their own. Still, although concerns about the potential break-up of the EU are understandable, the union will likely hold together.

Brexit will deal a huge blow to the international prestige and self-confidence—whatever is left of it—of the European project. European leaders may heed the populists and the lessons of Brexit by placing more restrictions on access to social benefits for EU migrants. Indeed, there is growing support for such policies across the political spectrum in Germany. If the EU is to regain its standing, its leaders must also get a grip on the refugee crisis and move away from its single-minded promotion of austerity, which has been both self-destructive and deeply unpopular across much of Europe. But ultimately, no other member state is likely to leave the union. For those in the eurozone, exit would simply be too costly. And new members in eastern Europe depend too heavily on EU funding to contemplate exit. Only in Sweden and Denmark is EU exit imaginable, although still unlikely because large majorities in both countries still believe they are better off inside the EU than out.

Above all, the union will not disintegrate because—despite all its current troubles—it remains, as German Chancellor Angela Merkel's chief of staff Peter Altmaier tweeted, "the best thing that happened to us in more than 200 years." If the EU didn't exist, European leaders would be trying to invent something like it. Certainly, many EU policies and institutions, above all the flawed regimes governing the eurozone and the Schengen zone, are in desperate need of reform (reform that some member governments have been blocking). But for all these faults, the EU has played a key role in promoting peace, prosperity, and democracy across Europe over six decades. Voters are frustrated with the EU, but most are even more frustrated with their national governments. Mainstream political parties across Europe remain deeply committed to the union, and we can expect European leaders to reaffirm that commitment in the days to come.

The United Kingdom has always been a reluctant member state, its marriage to Europe one of convenience, not love.

Late to join the European Economic Community, ambivalent from the start, and constantly demanding and securing opt-outs from the euro and the Schengen free-movement zone, the United Kingdom has been drifting away from the union for years. Even as the country held its European partners at arm's length, those partners have sought to embrace it. Citizens across Europe overwhelmingly supported the United Kingdom remaining in the EU, as did their leaders.

Luxembourg leading the pack in hoping the Brits stay in. (edging out Estonia) pic.twitter.com/vMRroWbE4n
— *ian bremmer (@ianbremmer) June 21, 2016*

In the waning days of the campaign, Continentals quite literally tried to show the United Kingdom their love with grassroots campaigns such as #HugaBrit that saw Europeans hugging British friends and pleading with them not to go. In the end, though, all the hugs and policy concessions were to no avail.

British politicians—and many voters—have blamed the European Union for their problems for years. Now they will have to find something new to bang on about as they deal with an economic downturn and increasing strains on their own political unity caused by the decision to leave. Soon enough, the British will discover whether they truly prefer life outside the union. Having divorced in haste, they may end up repenting at leisure.

R. DANIEL KELEMEN is Professor of Political Science and Law at Rutgers University.

Brexit's False Democracy

What The Vote Really Revealed

Kathleen r. Mcnamara

Demonstrators gesture outside the Houses of Parliament during a protest aimed at showing London's solidarity with the European Union following the recent EU referendum, in central London, Britain, June 28, 2016.

Referenda are terrible mechanisms of democracy. As a case in point, the recent British referendum over the United Kingdom's membership in the EU was a reckless gamble that took a very real issue—the need for more open and legitimate contestation in the EU—and turned it into a political grotesquerie of shamelessly opportunistic political elites. The raucous debate over the United Kingdom's continued membership in the EU was riven with lies and misrepresentations, some of which are now being explicitly rolled back by Brexit advocates; even the British press rues its bombastic support for the Leave side. Unfortunately, many British voters appear not to have known exactly what the EU is, validating other recent research demonstrating a lack of factual knowledge about the union.

Observers of the referendum should therefore be wary about drawing conclusions about broader globalization efforts, the Western order, the inevitability of the rise of populist anti-immigration parties, or the viability of the EU project overall. The answer to the breathless question posed in the New York Times on Sunday—"Is the post-1945 order imposed on the world by the United States and its allies unraveling, too?"—is simple. No, it is not. And yet the emotions and cultural chasms brought to bear in the Brexit vote cannot and should not be ignored.

Brexit's real lesson is that there is a consequential divide between cosmopolitans who view the future with hope and those who have been left behind and have seen their economic situations and ways of life deteriorate. The same story may well play out in the United States and elsewhere, with important electoral effects. But the Brexit story also speaks to the uniqueness of the EU as a new kind of polity with a profound impact on the lives of all within it. History has shown that the development of new political formulations rarely goes smoothly. The divisions between those who can imagine a better life in the new system and those who cannot will likely continue to drive politics in the EU and elsewhere for years to come.

DYLAN MARTINEZ / REUTERS

A demonstrator stands outside the Houses of Parliament during a protest aimed at showing London's solidarity with the European Union following the recent EU referendum, in central London, Britain, June 28, 2016.

CLASS CONSCIOUS

Although the Brexit referendum was a highly imperfect form of democratic representation, the emotions voiced by Leave voters were very real. They echo important and valid feelings of other populations across the Western democracies. There are two worlds of people, as analysis of Brexit voting patterns clearly indicated, that are divided in their experiences and their visions of the future. Educational attainment, age, and national identity decisively determined the vote. Younger voters of all economic backgrounds and those with a university education voted overwhelmingly in favor of Remain. Older voters, the unemployed, and those with a strong sense of English national identity sought to leave.

The fight over Brexit is a reflection of the social exclusion that arises in a world of stark economic inequality.

One way of thinking about the division is to see it as cosmopolitan versus parochial thinking, rooted in deeper social and economic trends that create their own cultural dynamics. Cosmopolitanism, a sense of belonging to a global community beyond one's immediate borders, requires confidence in one's place in the world and implies a hope about the future beyond the nation-state. The parochial view is tinged with fear about that future and a sense that societal transformation will leave the common voter behind. In part, that fear reflects the opening of markets, but it is equally due to changes in technology and broader shifts in capitalism away from protection of both the middle and the working classes. These shifts can't be blamed solely on globalization; they also have much to do with domestic politics and policy decisions. In the United Kingdom and elsewhere, political choices have accelerated deindustrialization while decimating social safety nets and doing little to put the brakes on rising inequality.

Given this harsh reality for the unemployed, the older, and the uneducated, the Remain campaign's warnings about the economic disaster of Brexit carried little weight; many voters believed that their opportunities were closed off long ago. The clever marketing of the Brexit campaign, including the mantras "Take Back Control" and "Breaking Point," spoke to very real senses of exclusion but offered few solutions; the reality is that British political dynamics, more than the EU's rules, have created the United Kingdom's social and economic problems.

The economic divide and the social effects of it pushed immigration to the forefront of the debate. Voters were right that immigration of both EU nationals and non-EU immigrants has risen tremendously, particularly since the financial crisis. Whereas other states within the EU have struggled with immigrants from Syria and Iraq, however, the United Kingdom has had a tiny number of asylum claims. And studies show that immigrants pay far more in taxes than they take out in benefits. Nevertheless, the underlying fears made such facts unimportant. Indeed, the areas with the most foreigners voted overwhelmingly for staying in the EU. They are regions already integrated into a new cosmopolitan world.

A taxi driver holds a Union flag, London, United Kingdom, June 24, 2016.

NEW POWER, NEW PROBLEM

The fight over Brexit is a reflection of the social exclusion that arises in a world of stark economic inequality. But the referendum should also be viewed in terms of a much longer history of political development and state building. The EU is far beyond a simple international organization or trade treaty, since it has accrued significant political authority across a wide range of areas. The rulings of the European Court of Justice, for example, supersede national law, and the laws of the EU have transformed everyday life in Europe, even as the Brussels bureaucracy and its fiscal presence remain tiny.

Historically, new political authorities have emerged and evolved in messy, ugly, and often violent ways. National projects of unification have involved coercion, civil wars, and the brutal exercise of power. Questions of federalism in the United States are still being fought today. Although the nation-state seems universal and natural, there have been many other forms of government in Europe alone: the Hapsburg monarchy, Italian city-states, the Holy Roman Empire, and the Hanseatic League, for example, have all come and gone. The EU, for all its faults, is an innovative new form, a polity in formation. Those under 45, and particularly those under 30, embrace it and see it as a natural and positive thing, a backdrop to their changed everyday lives that creates more opportunities than it closes down.

Given history's guide, we should not be surprised that the deepening of the EU has created a backlash. But we can be appalled by the craven opportunism and lack of political leadership in the United Kingdom and on the European continent in guiding this development. The EU will only work if all its citizens can imagine themselves part of a cosmopolitan, thriving democratic polity, one that balances local, national, and EU powers and creates economic opportunity. Listening to those on both sides of the cultural divide, and working to ease the economic inequality that underlies the division between the hopeful and the excluded, is the only way forward for the EU—and the rest of us.

KATHLEEN R. McNAMARA is a Professor at Georgetown University and the author of *The Politics of Everyday Europe: Constructing Authority in the European Union*.

© Foreign Affairs

The Roots of Brexit

1992, 2004, and European Union Expansion

PETER HALL

The Union Jack and the European Union flag are seen flying in the British overseas territory of Gibraltar, historically claimed by Spain, June 27, 2016, after Britain voted to leave the European Union in the EU Brexit referendum.

In their quest for the Conservative leadership, two rival Eton schoolboys have managed to take the United Kingdom out of the European Union—the first by calling for a referendum in 2013 in order to consolidate his hold over the leadership, and the second by joining the leadership of the Vote Leave campaign in order to hasten his rival's downfall. As Alex Salmond, the former leader of the Scottish National Party who knows a thing or two about referendums said, the point of a such a poll is to change things: it was daft of David Cameron to mount one when he planned to fight for the status quo. And it was cynical of Boris Johnson to use the opportunity for political gain. In this lamentable drama, both have much to answer for.

However, the two had help from many quarters, not least the halfhearted support for the Remain campaign from a Labour leadership ambivalent about the neoliberal capitalist engine that the EU has become and nervous about seeming to support immigration when so many of their traditional voters do not. Nigel Farage, the man-in-the-street leader of the United Kingdom Independent Party, contributed a willingness to play the race and immigration cards when the more delicate political tastes of some Conservatives held them back from doing so.

In a contest that saw a 52 percent vote to leave (and turnout was high at 72 percent), the vehicle for victory was a virulent populist nationalism, stirred up by a campaign laden with wild and inaccurate claims that 80 million Turks were on the brink of gaining EU membership and that a British contribution to the EU of 350 million pounds ($460 million) a week might otherwise be spent on the National Health Service. The Thatcherite Tories who have long disliked the EU saw the main issue as one of restoring British sovereignty, but focus groups revealed that few ordinary voters had any idea what sovereignty means. In fact, the majority of Brexit voters cared much more about immigration.

KACPER PEMPEL / REUTERS

Rates of currencies, including British Pound, are displayed after Brexit referendum on an electronic board at a currency exchange in Warsaw, Poland June 24, 2016.

In that respect, the roots of the referendum result lie in two historical developments—one in 1992 and the other in 2004. The 1992 Maastricht Treaty mandated the creation in 1999 of an EU monetary union, but the agreement left the EU without the institutions for sharing risks among the member states needed to help the union weather crises. When the Greek economy went into a tailspin, an EU in disarray had to cobble together a series of half measures through torturous negotiations that severely damaged its reputation for competence and has still failed to restore growth on the continent.

Of course, the creation of the euro was not unique as far as EU processes go. European negotiators often settle for a compromise that takes integration one step further, knowing that side effects from the inadequacies of that compromise will force future institution building. That process has created a unique transnational entity. But the euro's travails left British voters (and many other Europeans) with the impression that the EU is a defective enterprise incapable of delivering prosperity. This sentiment took the wind out of the sails of the Remain campaigners, who found it difficult to make the case for Europe as a noble aspiration on an island long suspicious of the continent. In the context of the euro crisis, claims that leaving the EU would damage the British economy rang hollow.

For those of us who have long thought that European influences bring out the better angels in the British nature, this is a sad moment.

The ground for this referendum result was also laid in 2004, when the EU agreed to accept eight east-central European states as members. Seen as an effort to guarantee democracy there, this was a generous move that won the European Union the 2012 Nobel Peace Prize. But because the EU's "four freedoms" include the right to free movement of workers, hundreds of thousands of workers flowed from the east into the United Kingdom, attracted by its universal language and open markets. Ironically, the British government had been a strong advocate for EU expansion, partly because an EU with a larger membership would be more like the free trade zone it favored than a political union. In recognition of this stance, Polish business leaders awarded Tony Blair, prime minister of the United Kingdom at the time, a golden statue. But when it joined the EU, GDP per capita in Poland was $12,830, compared with $33,640 in the United Kingdom; and by 2015 there were 790,000 Poles working in the United Kingdom, more than the entire population of Krakow.

Most studies show that immigration has been beneficial for the United Kingdom, which would otherwise have a shrinking population. It generates economic demand and jobs that might not otherwise exist. Across the regions of the United Kingdom, increases in immigration do not seem to have reduced the employment opportunities or pay of British-born workers. But perceptions are everything in politics and, fed by hysterical stories in the tabloids, most people think the United Kingdom has three times more EU migrants than it does.

WHAT NOW?

For now, it is difficult to say what will come next, not least because the Vote Leave campaign was riddled with contradictions. With respect to the country's relations with Europe, the Leave side claimed that the United Kingdom could secure access to the single market while retaining control over immigration. But in line with its arrangements with Norway and Switzerland, the EU is likely to make full access to that market contingent on the right to free movement of labor and perhaps some continuing contribution to EU budgets. Faced with surveys that show considerable support for similar referendums in other member states, EU leaders will realize that if a state can vote to exit and then negotiate a good deal, the very existence of the EU will be threatened. Perhaps that is why Cameron and Johnson have said they will hold off invoking Article 50 triggering an exit from the EU until the fall, thereby delaying any unpleasant revelations about what is on offer until after a new Conservative leader is chosen and any general election contingent on that has been held.

TOBY MELVILLE / REUTERS

A bus carries commuters as it travels over Waterloo Bridge in London, Britain, June 24, 2016.

In terms of domestic politics, the Leave campaign was an unholy alliance, initiated by a Conservative political elite interested in gaining sovereignty in order to deregulate the economy—despite support in the business community for the EU—but its margin of victory was provided by traditional Labour voters interested in more jobs, higher wages, and better public services. Brexit is unlikely to deliver what they want. Credible estimates suggest that in the short term, it will depress investment and growth. In the longer term, only the most rabid free marketeers can believe that further deregulation in an economy already dominated by flexible markets will generate new jobs. The total number of migrants from the EU in the United Kingdom is unlikely to decline much, since three-quarters of them have been in the United Kingdom long enough to qualify for permanent residence. Future flows may fall, but many small businesses in the service sector could go under as they struggle to fill the low-wage jobs on which their existence depends. Perhaps we will return to the days when Australians rather than Europeans served much of the beer sold in London pubs.

According to most estimates, the net gain to the United Kingdom of no longer contributing to the EU budget will be barely a third of the sums claimed by the Vote Leave campaign; and there is real uncertainty about how those funds will be spent. A large proportion of the EU funds sent to the United Kingdom went to the country's most depressed regions. Unless those are replaced from public coffers, the adverse effects of Brexit may be greatest in precisely those regions that supported it most strongly.

The referendum vote was won on a wave of public anger sweeping through the northern cities and countryside left out of the prosperity that integration into a global economy brought to London. Their anger could become all the greater when people discover that Brexit was largely a costly gamble with their futures. The Scottish Nationalist Party already intends to use the vote as the basis for another referendum on Scottish independence that it may well win, thereby leaving Cameron as the prime minister who broke up the United Kingdom. The Labour Party is not in much better shape, facing the dilemma of how to hold together an electoral coalition composed of sociocultural professionals who favor immigration and closer ties to Europe and working-class voters who are apprehensive about both. This referendum has brought to the surface deep divisions within the United Kingdom that will not be easily resolved, because rather than dividing the main parties, they cut through the middle of each of them.

For those of us who have long thought that European influences bring out the better angels in the British nature, this is a sad moment. At the time of the United Kingdom's last EU referendum in 1975, when two-thirds of the electorate voted to remain, Prime Minister Harold Wilson, himself no fan of integration, is reported to have said that he voted for membership because a loss would lead to the "wrong people" running the United Kingdom. Today, it is unclear who will now run the country or in what direction they will take it. It is not easy to put the genie of populist nationalism back into its bottle, and the contradictory promises of those who have won this referendum may well come back to haunt them.

PETER A. HALL is Krupp Foundation Professor of European Studies at Harvard University and a Centennial Professor at the London School of Economics.

The Irish Question

The Consequences of Brexit

HENRY FARRELL

A scrabble board spells out Brexit in Dublin, Ireland, May 2016.

The United Kingdom's historic decision to leave the EU has stunned Brussels and sent shock waves through Europe. The Scottish government has threatened to hold a second referendum on independence, jeopardizing the kingdom's unity. And in Ireland, the vote threatens to derail a fragile peace process and undermine a recent economic recovery.

Over the past four decades, the EU has transformed Ireland's relationship with the United Kingdom. Before both countries joined the bloc, in 1973, Ireland had achieved political but not economic independence. Its economy was rural and underdeveloped, leaving it reliant on British markets for its products. In the words of the French author Jean Blanchard, Ireland was an "island behind an island," its ties with its larger neighbor defined by a combination of supplication and resentment.

EU membership drew the poison out of the relationship. It provided Ireland with new markets and a fresh political forum in which it remade its partnership with the United Kingdom and its European neighbors. Over a period of a few decades, Ireland's agricultural economy was transformed into a postindustrial one, undergoing, in quick succession, a massive economic boom, a nasty crash, and a partial recovery. As Ireland grew, it stopped defining its identity solely in relation to the United Kingdom and instead began to see itself as a small, successful northern European state.

Ireland did not have to choose between Europe and the United Kingdom, since the latter was also a member of the EU. Sometimes, Ireland was constrained by its larger neighbor, as when it declined to join the EU's Schengen scheme for border-free travel—despite the Irish government's desire to do so—on the grounds that it already had a similar arrangement with the United Kingdom, which did not want to join the Schengen area. Usually, however, the tradeoffs were uncomplicated and easy to accommodate.

After last week, however, Ireland will no longer be able to have it both ways. If it wants to maintain good ties with the EU—and all indications suggest that it does—it will have to disentangle itself from the United Kingdom.

The Irish government did what it could to persuade the United Kingdom to stay in the EU; at the same time, it quietly prepared for a possible Brexit and has already announced contingency plans to manage changes over the short run.

However, Ireland also faces broader challenges, depending on the terms of any deal the United Kingdom strikes with the EU after its departure.

If Ireland wants to maintain good ties with the EU—and all indications suggest that it does—it will have to disentangle itself from the United Kingdom.

The most immediate problems involve Northern Ireland. After Brexit, the western border of the EU will cut straight through Ireland. Today, the border between Ireland and Northern Ireland is largely invisible, meandering along hedges and rural byways and sometimes cutting through farms.

In the future, border controls will have to be tougher. This may be a tall order: the British government will have a hard time maintaining control in the so-called bandit country of South Armagh, for example, where Irish nationalists have traditionally despised its presence. Sinn Fein, the political arm of the Irish Republican Army, has already started to argue that there should be no border between Ireland and Northern Ireland as part of its campaign for a united island. These pressures may destabilize the uncertain peace between nationalists, who are mostly Roman Catholic and want Northern Ireland to join Ireland, and unionists, who are mostly Protestant and want Northern Ireland to remain a part of the United Kingdom. Radical republicans, who have never been reconciled to peace, may turn again to large-scale violence.

CLODAGH KILCOYNE / REUTERS

A bar in Dublin has specially made a Brexit beer for the results of the British EU Referendum called "Big Mistake" in Ireland, June 2016.

In the past, European largesse helped to support peace in Northern Ireland, providing regional development and agricultural funds and funding reconciliation efforts. Ireland and the United Kingdom will find it difficult to replicate some of these efforts on their own. The EU has funded the Prison to Peace project, for example, a meeting group for formerly imprisoned paramilitaries that has encouraged dialogue among former enemies. Given renewed austerity measures, it will be hard for the Irish or British government to step in and provide such support when the EU withdraws.

What's more, the EU provided a space for former political rivals to get to know one another. The 1998 Good Friday Agreement, which led to peace in Northern Ireland, noted that Ireland and the United Kingdom were partners in the EU, as guaranteed in the European Convention on Human Rights.

Nationalists in Northern Ireland now worry that Brexit will weaken relations between it and Ireland and fear that the United Kingdom will soon withdraw from the European Convention.

A second set of problems involves the economy. The United Kingdom remains Ireland's most important export market. If the EU drives a tough deal with Britain after its exit, trade is likely to be disrupted. Depending on the exact terms of the deal, trade between Ireland and the United Kingdom could be subject to significant tariff and non-tariff barriers, damaging the Irish economy. Ireland's recent partial recovery has given the government sufficient leeway to ease austerity measures and increase spending. Brexit will likely put such progress on hold.

Of course, the United Kingdom's departure from the EU may also create opportunities for Ireland. London's financial sector is aghast at Brexit, since it may mean that British firms will no longer be allowed to use "financial passports" to export financial services to EU customers. This may lead some companies to relocate their activities to Dublin, which is English-speaking, has well-educated workers, and already has a significant financial services sector. However, the Irish government will have to invest in better transportation and communications infrastructure and build new housing in Dublin if it is to make a strong bid for new business. This may be difficult in uncertain economic conditions.

Finally, Brexit has complicated the already complex relationship between British and Irish citizenship. Ireland and the United Kingdom share a common travel area, making it easy for Irish and British citizens to live in each other's countries and vote in most of each other's elections. Irish residents of the United Kingdom, for example, were entitled to vote in the Brexit referendum. Under the Good Friday Agreement, anyone born in Northern Ireland is entitled to Irish citizenship, as is anyone who has at least one Irish grandparent.

After the Brexit vote, a flood of British citizens, worried about losing the benefits they enjoyed as EU citizens, have rushed to apply for Irish citizenship. The Northern Irish politician Ian Paisley, Jr., has encouraged his constituents to apply for Irish passports while they still can. Meanwhile, Ireland's foreign minister is begging U.K. residents to hold off from applying so as not to overwhelm the passport system.

For now, Ireland can try to square its two objectives—staying committed to Europe while maintaining strong ties with its most important neighbor—by influencing the exit deal the EU strikes with the United Kingdom. Although Ireland's voting strength is limited by its size, it may be able to play a valuable intermediary role. The United Kingdom will be eager to have a friend on the other side of the bargaining table. Ireland can informally represent the British position to Europe and vice versa. This will, in turn, allow it to advocate for its own interests. Ireland will likely want a deal that is favorable to the United Kingdom on trade issues, but that limits the consequences for the free movement of people of British anti-immigrant sentiment.

THE DISUNITED KINGDOM

When the United Kingdom leaves the EU, its own union may also dissolve. British national identity is a recent historical construct that may now be falling apart. Scotland's government is already talking about holding a second referendum on independence. And Northern Ireland voted in favor of remaining in Europe, although it is unlikely that a majority of Northern Irish voters will want independence or reunification with Ireland anytime soon.

As the United Kingdom's constitutional fabric threatens to unravel, Ireland may have an important role to play.

As the United Kingdom's constitutional fabric threatens to unravel, Ireland may have an important role to play in the institutions that will shape the region's future. Ireland and Northern Ireland already hold regular North-South Ministerial Councils, in which they cooperate on policy areas such as health, the environment, and transportation. The British-Irish Council—sometimes called the Council of the Isles—provides a forum in which Ireland, the United Kingdom, and the administrations of Northern Ireland, Scotland, and Wales meet to discuss issues of common interest, including environmental and energy policy.

In the short term, Brexit is likely to disrupt these arrangements. Cooperation will be far harder when some members are governed by EU rules and others are not. Over the longer term, however, these institutions might be transformed. For example, if Scotland votes for independence, a revamped Council of the Isles could assume a critical role in managing relations between the newly independent state and the United Kingdom, as well as providing opportunities to reshape relationships with Northern Ireland and Ireland.

Demonstrators take part in a protest aimed at showing London's solidarity with the European Union following the recent EU referendum, in London, June 2016.

In the worst-case scenario—if the United Kingdom ends up with only a limited economic and political relationship with the EU—Ireland's future will be compromised. It will have to make difficult choices about its border with Northern Ireland, economic policy, and citizenship. Opting for stronger relations with the United Kingdom in any one of these areas will damage relations with Europe, and vice versa.

Yet if the Irish government is able to shape the EU's deal with the United Kingdom—as well as the future of the kingdom itself—it may well transform its long-term relationships with both the United Kingdom and Europe for the better.

Henry Farrell is Associate Professor of Political Science and International Affairs at George Washington University's Elliott School of International Affairs. Follow him on Twitter @henryfarrell.

Scotland After Brexit

Will It Leave the United Kingdom?

JOHN CURTICE

Nicola Sturgeon, the First Minister of Scotland, smiles during a EU referendum remain event, at Edinburgh airport in Scotland, June 22, 2016.

When Scotland went to the polls in September 2014 to decide whether it wanted to become an independent country, Alex Salmond, Scotland's first minister at the time, called the ballot a "once in a generation" opportunity. If the country rejected the proposition, as it eventually did by 55 to 45 percent, then his party, the Scottish National Party (SNP), would, he said, honor that decision for the foreseeable future.

However, the recent Brexit referendum has given new life to the debate about Scottish independence. Although the United Kingdom voted to leave the EU by 52 to 48 percent, Scotland voted by 62 to 38 percent to remain.

Unsurprisingly, the current SNP first minister, Nicola Sturgeon, and her colleagues called it a "democratic affront" that votes cast in England could take Scotland out of the EU against its will. From their perspective, the U.K.-wide decision to leave the EU perfectly illustrates how being part of the United Kingdom limits Scotland's ability to determine its own affairs. As a result, the Scottish government is now trying to establish whether and how Scotland could retain its membership of the EU. It has convened a council of experts to advise on the options, and Sturgeon herself has already gone to Brussels to assess the lay of the land.

One suggestion is that Scotland could stay in the EU even if it is still part of a United Kingdom that has left. So far, though, nobody has demonstrated how that might be possible. The EU is, after all, a bloc of states. The only real option, then, looks to be for Scotland to leave the United Kingdom and secure membership of the EU as an independent state.

There are three potential hurdles that get in the way of this option, however. The first is public opinion. While the 45 percent level of support for independence recorded in the 2014 independence referendum has shown no sign of receding— indeed, it averaged 47 percent in opinion polls conducted before the Brexit referendum—this still left independence supporters in the minority. The crucial question is whether the British vote to leave the EU has upset enough Scottish voters to create a majority in favor of independence.

CLODAGH KILCOYNE / REUTERS

Scotland's Edinburgh Castle rock is illuminated with a sign to "Vote Remain" in the EU, June 21, 2016.

Polls conducted before the EU referendum suggested that the United Kingdom's vote for <u>Brexit</u> would result in a four- to five-point increase in support of independence, just enough to create a small majority in favor. Now, three polls conducted immediately after the referendum have estimated that support for independence has, indeed, increased to 52 to 54 percent. Still, such figures are well short of the 60 percent threshold that the SNP itself has previously indicated it would like to see before holding a second referendum. At the moment, holding a second ballot still looks like quite a risky option for the SNP.

The second potential hurdle facing the SNP is securing the legal authority to hold a second ballot. Scotland's constitutional status is one of the issues that is still in the preserve of the British Parliament in London rather than the responsibility of the devolved Scottish Parliament in Edinburgh. The September 2014 referendum was held after London had delegated the Scottish Parliament a time-limited authority to hold a referendum. That right has now expired.

It is open to doubt whether the next British prime minister and government would be willing to authorize a second Scottish independence referendum. It is true that before the 2014 referendum it was suggested that the Scottish Parliament might be able to hold, on its own authority, a referendum on whether the Scottish government should seek to open talks with the British government on Scotland's independence. But even if such a referendum avoided a challenge in the courts, the British government would not be under any obligation to honor the outcome.

The third and final hurdle is the most important one. How will the EU respond to an attempt by Scotland to become independent in order to retain its position inside the EU? The EU could say, as then President of the European Commission José Manuel Barroso suggested before the 2014 referendum, that an independent Scotland would have to apply for membership just like any other new applicant. And it might even have to wait years before securing admission. In that case, the SNP's prospects for a victorious second referendum would be significantly diminished.

Nicola Sturgeon in Edinburgh, Scotland, April 2015.

On the other hand, the EU might signal that it would allow an independent Scotland to be fast-tracked into membership and perhaps even to take over the United Kingdom's current membership. In that event, Sturgeon's chances of winning a referendum would be much greater.

This will not be an easy choice for the EU. Some of its members, most notably Spain, are concerned that cries for autonomy within their own countries (such as in Catalonia) will be emboldened if Scotland becomes independent. Indeed, Spanish Prime Minister Mariano Rajoy has already expressed his opposition to any EU talks with the Scottish government. On the other hand, it may seem hypocritical for the EU to reject Scotland's quest to stay in the union given that it has expressed its wish to do so through a democratic ballot.

Either way, Scotland's future may very well rest on whether the EU decides to extend a helping hand to Sturgeon or not.

JOHN CURTICE is Professor of Politics, University of Strathclyde, Glasgow.

© Foreign Affairs

The Swiss Model

Why It Won't Work For the United Kingdom

Lukas Kaelin

REUTERS

After the Brexit referendum, it became clear that the people had spoken. But in the days that followed, it also became clear that no one knew what had been said. And nowhere is this more apparent than with the leaders of the "Out" campaign who seem to have no real plan on how to actually leave the bloc and organize the United Kingdom's relationship with the European Union thereafter. Boris Johnson's surprise exit from the race to replace Prime Minister David Cameron, who announced his resignation following the vote, on top of the Labour Party establishment coup against its leader, Jeremy Corbyn, adds to this feeling of insecurity. Some observers have raised the option of the Swiss model. And there are certainly parallels worth considering, even if landlocked Switzerland has never attempted to join the EU and the island kingdom may soon be put out to sea.

Nearly a quarter century ago, in December, 1992, Switzerland held its own "In–Out" referendum. It was on whether to join the European Economic Area (EEA), which the Swiss government branded as a "training camp" for full membership into the European community and which, it argued, would come without any option for an exit. A small majority of the voters, prioritizing the protection of national sovereignty and fearing that the country would lose its cherished reputation for political neutrality if absorbed by the European Union, ticked "Out." For this group of voters, the expected economic benefits from joining and the possible geopolitical fallout from remaining out of the economic bloc, were less important.

In the last two decades, Switzerland has twisted itself in circles to strike different economic and political deals with the EU without actually becoming a member. It has even joined, among other treaties, the controversial Dublin Regulation requiring European countries to take in asylum-seekers wherever they first land. Switzerland also negotiated a deal with the EU that made it a member of the Schengen area, which effectively abolished Swiss sovereignty over its borders. Switzerland has never adopted the euro, and yet it is a de-facto currency in many regions of the country. And over the years, Switzerland has effectively participated in the creation of a European single market that guarantees the free movement of goods, capital, services, and people. Only in 2014 did the Swiss hold a popular vote demanding the restriction of immigration, but negotiations with EU leaders turned out to be next to impossible because restricting immigration would also lead to Brussels' withdrawal from key bilateral agreements. After the Brexit decision, it is very unlikely that Switzerland will reach an agreement over this issue, at least within the three-year period set by the Swiss referendum.

The Swiss model is not a viable plan for the United Kingdom or other countries curious about life outside the union. Switzerland has never joined the EU (and so never had to negotiate an exit). In view of Brussel's fear of protracted insecurity and a domino effect of other countries asking to leave the union, the British government is in a more difficult position to negotiate an exit. Furthermore, time constraints—invoking article 50 of the European Treaty that allows for two years tops for leave negotiations—do not favor the United Kingdom's bargaining position, as trade negotiation requires intense preparation that may be difficult, if not impossible, to achieve within such an amount of time. After all, the trade deal between Canada and the EU took seven years of negotiations and it is still unclear whether it will take effect.

If the United Kingdom were to follow the Swiss example, it would still have to follow all of the rules of the EU without being able to veto the bad ones.

Kevin Coombs / Reuters
The Big Ben clock tower in London, Britain, June 29, 2016.

Switzerland is also geopolitically insignificant. It is not a member of NATO and does not play an active role in global military conflicts. Its "permanent neutrality" gives it a role in security and peace negotiations and allows it to trade without regard to political affiliation. But, as a comparably small country surrounded by four large EU nations, it is radically economically dependent on the European Union. More than 50 percent of all Swiss exports go to EU countries, and almost 75 percent of all imports into Switzerland come from EU countries. That is why Switzerland has every reason to play nice with the EU.

The United Kingdom has equally vital interests in continuing its trade relations with the EU, which amount to about 50 percent of its imports and exports, respectively. The Swiss model shows that it is certainly feasible to reach a strong bilateral trade agreement, but there are tradeoffs for doing so, namely obliging Brussels on immigration, which was at the heart of the Leave campaign. In Switzerland's case, it became clear that becoming part of the single European market would mean accepting the free movement of people. When it comes to enforcing bilateral treaties with the EU, Switzerland is habitually forced to agree to laws decided by the union, in which it has no say, in order to keep trade unhindered. Right now Switzerland has to pay a "toll," as the EU critics call it: The Swiss are providing the Eastern EU members with $1.32 billion over ten years (from 2007 to 2016) in economic aid, which is set to be renewed beyond this year. Given that the Leave campaign promised to save the country money by leaving the EU, such an agreement would not sit well with the British people.

So in essence, if the United Kingdom were to follow the Swiss example, it would still have to follow all of the rules of the EU without being able to veto the bad ones;

the country's bargaining position is hardly better than Switzerland's. Of course, it can use London as leverage. It would hurt Europe too, at least temporarily, if the international financial hub were suddenly shut out of the single market. U.S. and European stock markets tumbled alongside the British one on Friday, and since the vote, global markets have lost $3 trillion. In Germany, the United Kingdom's third-biggest export market, Chancellor Angela Merkel has, unsurprisingly, called for an unrushed, reasoned approach. The United Kingdom is also eyeing a new regulation, slated to go into effect in 2018 (which is right around when Leave negotiations would wrap up) that would allow it to retain most of its "passporting" rights, which give its financial sector unfettered access to the EU market. But the United Kingdom has more to lose as Frankfurt prepares to accommodate a large portion of the London banking business should the British government invoke Article 50. And in general, EU market access would almost certainly mean accepting the freedom of movement rules and contributing to the EU budget.

Given the novelty of Brexit and the size and importance of the United Kingdom, it is difficult to make any meaningful predictions about the upcoming exit negotiations. Over the next few weeks, London and Brussels will begin discussions on how to translate the current chaos into sensible policies, but whether that means joining the EEA (like Norway and Iceland), following a bilateral Swiss model, or carving out an entirely new path is yet to be determined.

LUKAS KAELIN is Assistant Professor at the Catholic Theological Private University Linz and Lecturer at the University of Vienna.

© Foreign Affairs

NATO After Brexit

Will Security Cooperation Work?

Frank J. Cilluffo and Sharon L. Cardash

U.S. army personal take part in the "Saber Strike" NATO military exercise in Adazi, Latvia, June 13, 2016.

Commentators have rushed to weigh in on the political and economic implications of the Brexit referendum. But the potential security effects are just as important. At risk are operational matters such as data and intelligence sharing. But also in question is something more fundamental: the relationships that allow security services to live and breathe. The United Kingdom, EU, and other partners will now have to redefine their security and intelligence relationships.

Such negotiations will take time. And before taking a seat at the table, all parties would be well served to think carefully through some of the critical strategic and tactical questions that will have to be addressed, even as they bear in mind that fissures among EU member states' law enforcement and intelligence communities predate the referendum and that adversaries are likely to seize any fragmentation as an opportunity to test resolve.

Europe's fracturing gives Russia a chance to push the envelope, as it has been doing in recent years in Ukraine and elsewhere. For months now, Russia has been testing the continental and transatlantic alliance by bringing difficult and potentially divisive issues to the fore. Recent Russian exercises, deployments, and rhetoric have seemed intended to probe the depth of the EU's and NATO's commitment to securing their borders.

Russian fighter craft have buzzed the edges of NATO airspace for months, trying to ascertain the limits of allied discipline and restraint. Beneath the sea, Russian submarines have been "aggressively operating near" the undersea cables that are instrumental to the functioning of the U.S. military and the world economy. In cyberspace, meanwhile, Russia has tried to destabilize foes through propaganda, including by depicting Germany as "a society in chaos because of migration." And pulling no punches, within hours of the British referendum, the mayor of Moscow stated that "without Great Britain in the EU, no one will so zealously defend the sanctions against us." In short, Brexit is effectively a gift to Russia, and it will likely keep on giving.

The Islamic State (also known as ISIS), too, has looked to weaken European unity and destabilize the West. In one issue of its newsletter, the group boasted that the Paris attack could lead to the "the weakening of European cohesion, including demands to repeal the Schengen Agreement." To this end, it is alarming that the planning for the latest ISIS attacks in Belgium and France spanned so many EU countries. The perpetrators shared information on everything from concepts to capabilities through complex networks that took advantage of gaps in information, intelligence, and cooperation, within and among allied security services. If anything, these attacks showed the need for Europe to come closer together, not further apart, via Brexit or otherwise.

EU entities such as Europol are tasked with Europe's security and intelligence portfolio and will lose the substantial assets, tangible and not, that the United Kingdom has brought to the table. The country's highly capable security and intelligence services have helped power EU efforts in this area, and even if the partners reach alternate arrangements (for access to data and so on), the United Kingdom will lose the ability to lead and influence from within. There is also the EU's relationship with NATO to keep in mind. It has always been a challenge to avoid duplication and inefficiency between the EU and NATO. But the potential for divergence between the two entities could be magnified now that the United Kingdom is no longer around to bridge the breach. Taking a hardheaded approach to threats—including those in the newest domain, cyberspace—the United Kingdom has worked in the past to focus European minds and resources on the most pressing issues, in a way that makes use of the complementarity between these security architectures. Whether this process will continue in practice, rhetoric aside, remains to be seen.

Historically, the United Kingdom has also acted as linchpin between Europe and the United States, cementing the security bond across the pond. Although some of the luster has worn off the special relationship, the fact remains that the United Kingdom has long served as a touchstone for the United States in its dealings with Europe writ large, and it remains the United States' closest European ally. With both countries now outside the EU bloc, and in the absence of a principal long-standing interlocutor, the United States could well find it harder to make its case to Europe on issues of critical importance. From the imposition of economic sanctions on Russia and Iran to the designation of Foreign Terrorist Organizations, the United States was instrumental in getting to the goal when differences within the EU existed.

At a more tactical level, Brexit could harm efforts to combat terrorism and organized crime. In both areas, data sharing is the coin of the realm. At the working level, law enforcement and intelligence authorities in different countries may well have robust and productive cross-border relationships, based on mutual trust and respect built up over time. But these ties can take policing only so far in the absence of formal agreements to underpin and authorize such exchanges. To maintain its present level of access, the United Kingdom would have to negotiate a host of bilateral arrangements with remaining EU member states, each with its own disposition, views, and possible sticking points on the matter.

Brexit comes at a time when European security is already under threat. Both state and nonstate actors are brazenly challenging Europe and it allies. Substantial uncertainty lies ahead for the United Kingdom, for the EU, and for the relationship of both to the United States. Reaching a new modus vivendi that maximizes safety and minimizes divisions is in the interest of all of the parties. Those responsible for defining, calibrating, and implementing this new equilibrium surely know as much. The challenge, however, will be to insulate and protect the law enforcement and intelligence domains from the political bluster and positioning that will surely accompany the negotiations.

FRANK J. CILLUFFO directs the George Washington University Center for Cyber & Homeland Security (CCHS) and served as Special Assistant to the President for Homeland Security immediately after 9/11. SHARON L. CARDASH is Associate Director of the CCHS and previously served as Security Policy Adviser to Canada's Minister of Foreign Affairs.

July 10, 2016

A Brexiteer's Celebration

A Conversation with Kwasi Kwarteng

TOBY MELVILLE / REUTERS

Kwasi Kwarteng as a candidate for parliament in London, March 2010.

"A rising star on the right," as the BBC has called him, Kwasi Kwarteng was elected to the British Parliament in 2010 as a member of the Conservative Party. The son of Ghanaian immigrants, he received a Ph.D. in economic history from Cambridge University and worked as an investment banker before entering politics. Kwarteng, a supporter of the United Kingdom's leaving the EU, spoke with Foreign Affairs deputy managing editor Stuart Reid in London on July 6.

Why did the people vote for Brexit?

The first issue, obviously, was immigration—and immigration as it's perceived, not so much in London or the southeast, but particularly in northern areas and agricultural areas. People feel that having 150,000 eastern Europeans coming in every single year, who can just come by mere virtue of the fact that they have EU citizenship, drove down wages. These are lower-paid people. And I always thought, Why would they vote to be in a system where, essentially, you're forcing people to compete with 150,000 extra workers every year, essentially driving wages down and diminishing the quality of life for a lot of these people? That's the perception. A lot of clever people talk about the "lump of labor fallacy" and all the rest of it, but there are lots of different economic theories involved. But the perception was what drove the politics, not the economic theory. In large parts of rural England—a town like Boston, which your own town of Boston is named after—the perception was that things were changing, life wasn't getting better for quote-unquote indigenous people, and they voted against that.

The second thing was there's also a nationalistic spirit to a lot of people in England. They felt that they wanted to get their country back. They wanted to take control. That was the phrase that the Vote Leave campaign used, and it was a highly effective one. They didn't like these foreigners in Brussels bossing them around. They have a sense of British exceptionalism, which they derived from their history and World War II and all those sorts of things.

Thirdly, there was a sense that they wanted to kick the political establishment. You saw this with the [Donald] Trump nomination in the primaries. They wanted to send a message to their political elite that they weren't going to be pushed around. They'd had enough.

If voters are actually wrong about the economic impact, do politicians have a duty to correct those perceptions?

This is one of the most extraordinary developments in this debate. We have a democracy. Every democracy in the history of the world will have had people losing elections saying, "The people were misinformed, the people were ignorant, the people didn't know about A, B, or C." That always happens. That's what losing an election feels like. No one who ever lost an election said, "The people were totally informed and totally accurate and made a rational choice and didn't vote for me." We have a democratic system. Now, if we didn't like that, we could have teams of experts and economists and smart people with a Ph.D., but we don't.

A lot of this is sour grapes. People are upset that they've lost and so they say the people were misinformed, the people were lied to, the people are dumb. I actually feel that people have a very acute sense of their own self-interest and they vote accordingly.

People are upset that they've lost and so they say the people were misinformed, the people were lied to, the people are dumb.

Do you think racism played any role in the vote?

I think a little bit. It would be absurd to say that it played absolutely no role whatsoever. I think you can understand it more broadly in terms of national identity, culture, a sense of pride. And we can't have it both ways. In the last few years, we've had a diamond jubilee, we've had a royal wedding, we've had the queen's 90th birthday, the London Olympics. This decade has been one of quite a lot of national feeling in Britain. We've had two royal babies being born; the succession has been secured. All this feeds into a mood.

TOBY MELVILLE / REUTERS

The UK Independence Party's Nigel Farage, the man behind Brexit, addresses supporters in London, June 2016.

What was your rationale for voting to leave?

I think that the EU [is] fairly corrupt. I think it's unaccountable. I think there's no real democratic transparency. There were these people called the five presidents—no one knew who they were or what they did.

There was a sense they were going down this integrationist route without really consulting the people. Something had to give. And I think the Brexit vote, actually, has made [other European countries] examine themselves more in terms of where their strategic direction lies.

A couple months ago, a Dutch friend of mine who is very pro-EU said to me, "Well, at least if Brexit does happen, we will have to think more closely about what it is we want out of the EU." In a way, we've jolted them into that debate. Either they will resolve that question and provoke reform or they won't, in which case we were probably right to leave. It's a very vulgar thing that my constituent said, but I was talking to someone in the pub, and he said, "I want to kick them up the arse." That was very much a feeling that a lot of ordinary voters felt.

Did you expect the financial turmoil that ensued?

We've made our decision and there's no way back to the status quo.

Let's talk about financial turmoil. I've seen financial turmoil. The FTSE 100 [the Financial Times Stock Exchange 100 Index] went from 6,900 at the end of 1999 to 3,300 at the beginning of 2003. I worked in the City when the FTSE lost about 52 percent in little more than three years. I've seen grinding bear markets.

Let's just see the fallout of this. There will be some readjustment, but it's very easy to get carried away with apocalyptic prognostications and prophecies. Yeah, there will be some uncertainty. But this is forever. This whole idea of having a second referendum or postponing Article 50 [the provision in the Lisbon treaty for withdrawing from the EU] indefinitely—that's not going to happen. We've made our decision and there's no way back to the status quo.

What's next in terms of process?

We will certainly get a new prime minister in September. I hope they invoke Article 50 perhaps in the first six months. And then from the beginning of 2017, we count down two years, and we should be out of the EU in 2019.

A demonstrator at a pro-EU rally in Trafalgar Square, June 2016.

What does Brexit mean for U.S.-British relations?

I don't think it means anything. We were in the EU for 43 years. We joined in '73, we voted to leave in 2016, we could be out in 2019. That's a 46-year period. I'm 41 years old. This isn't a very long time. And the special relationship is something that's evolved over decades, if not a couple of centuries. When was the Mayflower—1620, right? Saying that ending our 43-year involvement [with] the EU is somehow going to fundamentally change this deep relationship between our two countries is completely unhistorical.

You're an economic historian. How do you look at Brexit through the lens of your field?

If you look at British trade patterns before the EEC [European Economic Community], certainly before the Second World War, the U.K. has always been a maritime power. The trade routes were extensive across the world. Britain's trade was global long before any other country's was, through industrialization, through empire. And the EEC skewed that natural relationship that we had with all the continents of the world. [French President Charles] de Gaulle made this point in '63 when he vetoed Britain's EEC membership. He said, "Look, the British are a maritime power. They've got incredibly complicated trade routes and trade links and a supply chain right across the world. This doesn't necessarily fit in with our continental view in terms of the single market we want to create." And I think future historians may well look back on the EEC/EU period as somewhat of an aberration in terms of the sweep of economic history.

A London cab driver celebrates Brexit, June 2016.

Which direction do you think Europe will go next? More integration and centralization or less?

This is a fundamental question, and I think in answering that question, you have to look at what's going to happen with the actual currency, because it seems to me that you have quite bad economic conditions, certainly in Greece and Italy and potentially in Spain and Portugal. These countries are in many ways suffering because of membership in the eurozone.

I think the eurozone can go one of two ways. You can have a common currency, which they already have, and then they might have to think about some sort of harmonized fiscal policy, because it was the failures of fiscal policy that led to the crisis, certainly in Greece. And a harmonized fiscal policy will require more integration. Then the countries that aren't in the eurozone, if the eurozone were to consolidate, would of necessity be further excluded from it. So I think Europe has to reform one way or the other, or the alternative is a looser federation. Maybe the eurozone splits off into different currency zones—I don't know.

What do you foresee for the future of the Conservatives?

I think the Conservatives will rally round. Obviously, we need to have a new leader, and a new prime minister. I think Theresa May, who is the home secretary, is in a very strong position to win. I hope she wins. Once she's in place and once we have a new government in place, we can stabilize the situation and move forward and deliver on Brexit.

People can look at the alternatives and say, "Actually, you know what? We'll go through a period of uncertainty so that we can secure something better at the end of it." That's the story of human progress.

Anything else you'd like to add?

There are moments of transition. You see that across the world. But that doesn't mean that the place you get to is worse. In some cases, it can be worse, but in many cases, it can be better. I'm amazed when Americans express concern. You guys fought a War of Independence that lasted six years. There was hyperinflation, there were bad things that happened, but at the end, you had an independent country.

Now, I'm not saying the EEC or EU is as bad as George III. But I am saying that people can look at the alternatives and say, "Actually, you know what? We'll go through a period of uncertainty so that we can secure something better at the end of it." That's the story of human progress.

Note: This interview has been edited and condensed.

© Foreign Affairs

A Remainer's Lament

A Conversation With Ed Balls

Britain's Shadow Chancellor of the Exchequer Ed Balls speaks at the Fabian Society's annual conference in London, January 2014.

A longtime member of the United Kingdom's Labour party, Ed Balls was elected to parliament in 2005 and served as shadow chancellor of the exchequer from 2011 to 2015. Before that, he was chief economic adviser to the Treasury and a columnist at The Financial Times. Now a senior fellow at the Harvard Kennedy School, Balls, who supported the Remain campaign, spoke with Foreign Affairs deputy managing editor Stuart Reid in London on July 6.

What were the motivations voters had for leaving the European Union?

There's been some big changes in our economies over 20 years as a result of globalization, and I don't think that either politicians or economists properly understood what those meant. One was that, 20 years ago when I was involved in making the Bank of England independent, we all thought that the biggest threat to stability was going to come from the government's mistakes regarding inflation. And then we had a global financial crisis in an era of low inflation, the consequences of which are still playing out economically and politically.

The second thing is, we thought globalization and technological change were going to impact, in particular, the wages and jobs of the unskilled, but it's really bitten into the wages and the incomes of people in the middle. You've seen in America and in Britain a big squeeze on the incomes of middle earners, and that's made people angry.

The third thing is, we thought globalization would be about capital markets and trade, and nobody foresaw globalization of people moving on this scale. When I was writing for The Financial Times 25 years ago, we thought the issue was going to be Polish workers in Poland undercutting British car workers in Britain. What nobody foresaw was economic migration happening on the scale that it has. The reason why in Britain we didn't have transitional controls on Eastern European migration in 2004 was that we didn't really think people were going to move.

Some have blamed the anti-immigrant backlash on the Labour Party's policies, beginning in the 1990s, that ramped up immigration. Is there any truth to that?

We've always been a country that has brought skilled people from around the world to work here. The City of London depends upon that. Labour did that while in government, but so had the previous Conservative government after Big Bang [the 1986 deregulation of British financial markets]. The mistake happened in 2004. We had just as a country decided not to join the single currency, the euro. I was at the Treasury, very involved in making sure we didn't join. Then, a year later, when the accession of the East European countries happened, we had the option of having transitional controls on migration, and we said no. We said no partly from a diplomatic, foreign policy point of view; having said no to the euro, we wanted to be pro-European.

But the second thing was that we got the forecasts wrong. The government thought the numbers would be in the tens of thousands, and it turned out to be in the hundreds of thousands. David Cameron, then the Conservative Prime Minister, who gave Labour a very hard time for not controlling immigration, said in his manifesto 10 that he would get net migration down to the tens of thousands. But he and didn't. Having promised to do it and then having failed, that led to cynicism that nothing can be done.

DYLAN MARTINEZ / REUTERS

Demonstrators take part in a protest aimed at showing London's solidarity with the European Union following the recent EU referendum in central London, United Kingdom, June 2016.

How much of this vote was a rejection of expertise?

Whether you look at the left or the right, populist arguments often use the same language: "The rules aren't fair. The system is rigged against you. You work hard and get an unfair deal. Somebody else is coming in and short-changing you, whether that is welfare cheats or multinational companies not paying their taxes. And when the elite, the establishment, the experts tell you this is the way it is, they're just trying to hoodwink you." We absolutely saw that language from the Leave campaign in exactly the same way as we see it from Donald Trump in the United States, or to some extent Jeremy Corbyn when he was fighting his Labour leadership campaign. The shocking thing is that the former Mayor of London, Boris Johnson, used those arguments, and the former Education Secretary, Michael Gove, used these arguments—even though in their previous jobs, they relied upon experts all the time.

But I'm afraid it is reflective of a broader cynicism across populations at the moment about politics and trust. It goes back to those fundamental assumptions we got wrong. People look at the global financial crisis and say, "You told us it was all going fine, and suddenly there was this massive banking crisis, and we've paid the price. You told us the market economy and globalization would make us better off, and I'm worse off." When you see those jarring disappointments, people do start to question authority and expertise.

Should those Americans who are worried about the prospect of a Donald Trump presidency draw any lessons from the Brexit vote?

Well, I'm very much hoping that we're not going to see a Donald Trump presidency. Although when I arrived in Harvard last September, many of my American friends said, "Donald Trump will be gone by October or November. That's what always happens. These people flare and then crash." And my reply was, "Well, that's what they said about Jeremy Corbyn."

YVES HERMAN / REUTERS

European Council President Donald Tusk (L) and European Commission President Jean-Claude Juncker wait for Macedonian President Gjorge Ivanov ahead of a meeting at the EU Council headquarters in Brussels, Belgium, February 2016.

The markets did not react well to the Brexit vote. What are we likely to see going forward?

I think it is now likely—not necessary, but likely—there will be a recession in Britain. At the moment, this is a British event, so we wouldn't expect to see big ver. But the large fall in the pound—its lowest level now in 30 years, a 20 percent t the dollar—says that people are thinking their investments are going to here. If we see a sustained period of companies changing their whether that's in real estate, manufacturing, or financial services—

then the long-term effects for the country could be more profound than simply gyrations in short-term markets.

For the United States, the issue is less, "Is Britain going to undermine the American economy?" and more, "Is what's happened in Britain an indication of a political trend that we might see repeated in the United States in the presidential election?" And that would be a much, much more serious economic event for the United States and the world.

What does Brexit mean for the future of U.S.–British relations?

Britain is a member of NATO, the G-7, and the G-20, and what's inevitably going to happen is that it is going to talk about those things more from outside the European Union. We've always been a good ally to our American partners. But I think they also knew that the partnership is much stronger and more effective if Britain is not simply part of a bridge across the Atlantic, but also a bridge to the European Union. We will be a less influential and less effective ally to the United States from outside the European Union, especially if we end up walking away from Europe entirely. My hope is that while we are going to leave the political EU, we will find a way in which we continue to be an important economic player in Europe. But if we choose to become a greater Albania, that's going be less interesting to our American friends, and rightly so.

What would you like to see happen next in terms of the procedure of decoupling from the EU?

There's a divide both in Britain and amongst our European partners about the right strategy. In London, the choice is likely to come down to whether this is really a divorce negotiation or whether this is about finding a new accommodation. I think that it's in Europe's as well as in Britain's interests to make the single market work while restricting freedom of movement. But if Europe insists that without free movement, you can't stay in the single market—I think that will be very difficult for Britain. But the Conservative Party and the country are going to work out which side of that divide they want to be on. I hope they reach an accommodation rather than just walk away.

But our European partners have got to make a choice, as well. [European Commission President] Jean-Claude Juncker said last week [essentially], "Good riddance. You made your decision, we can't let anybody else follow you; so, we want to get this done and get you out." An alternative view is saying, "This could be very damaging for Europe as well. Let's try and find an accommodation which keeps Britain as part of the wider family, even if it's outside the union."

Do you see Europe going in the direction of more integration or less?

If this is a reflection of a frustration about politics and government, stability and wages, and migration in the eyes of the British voters, all of those issues arise across the European Union. The eurozone has clearly not been an economic success. Migration and the refugee crisis are impacting politics across the European Union. Concerns about leadership and elites and expertise—you'll hear exactly the same things said in Austria, Sweden, Denmark, and France as in Britain. Sometimes, our European colleagues find it easier to dismiss such problems as being British problems or Anglo-Saxon ones, whereas I think these are problems that concern developed countries across the world. They need to stand back and learn some lessons. If they do, that will help us. A more functioning, deeper, more integrated eurozone would be good for the world economy and good for Europe. We were never going to be part of that; we were always in some sense going to be on the outside. But I think finding a way to make the single market deeper while managing migration more effectively is necessary.

I was at a meeting a couple of days ago with colleagues from the economic and foreign policy establishment, and the question was asked, "If there were a vote on TTIP [the Transatlantic Trade and Investment Partnership], how many populations across Europe would vote for the agreement?" The view was almost none. That is a problem, because if we react against deepening our economic cooperation, we'll end up impoverishing ourselves.

Your own party now appears to be in disarray. What does the future hold for Labour?

Over the last 18 months, anybody who told you that they had any idea of what to foresee was a fool. It's been total chaos. There's huge frustration within sections of Labour supporters and Labour MPs that the leadership and Jeremy Corbyn didn't campaign for an In vote effectively, which is a reflection of the fact that he's never really believed in the European Union over the last 40 years. That divide between the cities and the towns is a very big one within Labour, because we have lots of heartland, small-town areas, old industrial areas, which are very different these days from an urban, diverse Britain.

But that's overlaid on a political crisis. The members of the party who choose a leader have become very disconnected from Labour voters. So you have a membership that has become much more leftwing, much more anti-capitalist, anti-globalization, anti-NATO, anti-market economy, and that's not where the British public is. In politics, you can lead by persuading people to change, but if you tell people they're wrong, then they don't tend to want to follow. The Labour leadership has spent the last year telling its members what they want to hear and the rest of the country that they're wrong. The members quite like it, and the rest of the country thinks, "What have you got to do with our lives?"

Note: this interview has been edited and condensed.

May's Brexit Mastery

Time for the United Kingdom to Move On

CAMILLE PECASTAING

Britain's Home Secretary Theresa May, who is due to take over as prime minister on Wednesday, waves as she leaves after a cabinet meeting at number 10 Downing Street, in central London, Britain July 12, 2016.

The quadrennial excitement of the Euro soccer competition, the green lawns of Wimbledon, and the racetrack at Silverstone provided three weeks of distraction from the consequences of the United Kingdom's June 23 referendum. Prime Minister David Cameron was resigning, yes, but nothing would happen until his successor was in place, and it would take months for the country's political parties, all in crisis, to select new leaders. Some supporters of staying in the European Union fancied using the lull to hold a second referendum to confirm the first, which was not binding. Demoralizing threats kept coming—from George Soros, from the IMF, from others—about the cost of withdrawal. Even the pro-Brexit camp seemed suddenly confused about the economic benefits of leaving the EU. Many started to imagine a withdrawal from the union pushed to such a distant future that it would never actually happen.

Time accelerated on July 12, though, when Tory Home Secretary Theresa May surged to the position of prime minister and declared unreservedly that she would implement Brexit. Her instincts may have been against it, but she promised that she would honor the vote and that she would be able to turn Brexit into a favorable arrangement for Britain. It was a stroke of political genius, first because the United Kingdom is a democracy and the vote ought to be acknowledged, and second because negotiations with the EU could be relatively easy and mutually beneficial.

NEIL HALL

Participants hold a British Union flag and an EU flag during a pro-EU referendum event at Parliament Square in London, Britain June 19, 2016.

The results of the Brexit referendum have opened the doors of power to May, an unsentimental politician with a career that reminds one of a Supreme Court judge— a role in which one displays competency without giving offense. In the campaign leading to the referendum, for example, she notoriously favored the United Kingdom's remaining in the EU but declined to burn political capital by defending her position. She is now similarly poised to give Britons their "exit" cake and allow them to eat the "remain" too.

Here, it is worth looking to two other European countries that passed on EU membership: Norway, with a GDP per capita close to $70,000; and Switzerland, with a GDP of $60,000. Not all economies are comparable—Norway lives off oil and fish—but the GDP per capita of the United Kingdom just exceeds $40,000. In other words, there is no absolute link between membership in the EU and national wealth. Furthermore, although they are non-members, Norway and Switzerland are deeply integrated in the regulatory framework of the EU, which facilitates their commerce with the region.

The new British prime minister should rush to invoke Article 50 of the Treaty on European Union.

The two cases offer a template for a post-Brexit United Kingdom, one that is still integrated economically with the continent. As for the cost of the divorce, a loss can simultaneously be a gain. Rewriting rules and regulations, and renegotiating deals will add up to thousands of billable hours for lawyers and accountants. European economies will absorb the costs and find new areas of growth, and May will come across as the champion of popular will. For such a rosy outcome, though, time is of the essence. The new British prime minister should rush to invoke Article 50 of the Treaty on European Union, which starts the process of secession. Rapid agreement on a framework between London and Brussels will soothe Britons and allow European public opinion to move on to other topics. The sooner the United Kingdom is out of European minds, and the EU is out of British minds, the sooner the noxious politics of Brexit can be laid to rest. By defusing the political question, a rapid framework agreement will leave bureaucrats and lawyers months, maybe years, to finesse behind closed doors the commercial and regulatory details. In the end, when it comes to economic integration, the EU-UK relationship may not look very different pre- and post-Brexit. And no one will care.

A demonstrator at a pro-EU rally in Trafalgar Square, June 2016.

After all, whether Brexit costs a quarter or half of a percentage point of GDP—or nets it—it is not consequential to most voters. The vote was more about the apparent end of a treasured way of life, about alien products in the supermarket, and about ethnic food where the fish and chips used to be. The Brexit result was aspirational, a nostalgic appeal to a past that can never be reclaimed, because the United Kingdom is already far more open and cosmopolitan than its voters wish it to be.

British parochialism finds echoes on the other side of the Channel, where European leaders, as a group, failed to sell the European way of life to their people. The union is now paying the price, but Brexit opens a window for those who remain to remedy political disaffection and reinvigorate the European project. Already, Emmanuel Valls, the French prime minister, and Matteo Renzi, his Italian counterpart, have declared their intention to push for further integration. Many more should join to emphasize the shared political and cultural destiny, and to convince the public that Europe is an identity, not just a fractional point of GDP growth.

In the same way that Europe is struggling to come to terms with what it is, politically and culturally and ethnically, May's more insular United Kingdom will have to find its own voice and self-image post-Brexit. The political task of reconciling an insular United Kingdom with itself, diverse as it is, will be far more arduous than negotiating the terms of future economic integration with the European Union. It remains to be seen whether that is a challenge that the new prime minister—or anyone else in her shoes—will be able to meet.

CAMILLE PECASTAING is Senior Associate Professor of Middle East Studies at Johns Hopkins University's School of Advanced International Studies.

CPSIA information can be obtained
at www.ICGtesting.com
Printed in the USA
LVHW101521180419
614687LV00010B/268/P